So you really want to learn

English
Prep
BOOK 2

So you really want to learn

English
Prep
BOOK 2

Susan Elkin

Series Editor: Nicholas Oulton M.A. (Oxon.)

www.galorepark.co.uk

Independent Schools
Examinations Board

GALORE PARK

Published by ISEB Publications, an imprint of Galore Park Publishing Ltd,
PO Box 96, Cranbrook TN17 4WS
www.galorepark.co.uk

Illustrations by Ian Douglass

Printed by The Bath Press

ISBN-13: 978 1 902984 66 7
ISBN-10: 1 902984 66 8

The publishers are grateful for permission to use extracts as follows:
Extract from CIRCUS LION from the Complete Poems of C. Day Lewis published by Sinclair-Stevenson (1992)
Copyright © 1992 in this edition The Estate of C. Day Lewis. Reprinted by permission of The Random House Group
Ltd; BBC news item JUMBO-SIZED PROTEST – permission sought: extract from LORD OF THE FLIES by William
Golding reproduced by permission of the author and the publishers Faber and Faber Ltd; extract from DEATH OF
AN AIRCRAFT from the Collected Poems of Charles Causley by kind permission of the author and the publishers
Macmillan; Daily Telegraph news article VILLAGERS PLUCKED FROM THE TORRENT © Telegraph Group Limited
2004; extract from NOUGHTS AND CROSSES by Malorie Blackman Copyright © Malorie Blackman by permission
of The Random House Group Ltd; the poem TELEPHONE CONVERSATION by Wole Soyinka Copyright © 1962 by
Wole Soyinka. Reprinted by permission of Melanie Jakson Agency, L.L.C.; extract from the Martin Luther King
speech I HAVE A DREAM reproduced by permission of Pollinger Limited and the proprietor; the poem CHRISTMAS
by John Betjeman reproduced by permission of John Murray Publishers; extract from THE WORDSWORTH
DICTIONARY OF SAINTS by Alison Jones by permission of Chambers Harrap Publishers Ltd; extract from
WALKABOUT by James Vance Marshall, retold by Gillian Porter Ladousse (first published as THE CHILDREN by
Michael Joseph 1959, Penguin Readers version published by Pearson Education 2000). Original Copyright © James
Vance Marshall, 1969. Text Copyright © Penguin Books, 2000; extract from LIFE IN A LIBERTY BODICE by
Christabel Burniston by kind permission of the author; the poem TIMOTHY WINTERS from the Collected Poems of
Charles Causley by kind permission of the author Charles Causley and the publisher Macmillan; extract from
WWW.LONDONTOURIST.ORG by kind permission of London Tourism; extract from RICE WITHOUT RAIN by
Minfong Ho Copyright © Minfong Ho by permission of AM Heath & Co Ltd on behalf of Minfong Ho; extract from
Christian Aid article INDIA BITTEN BY DROUGHT, BUT LACK OF RAIN IS NOT THE ONLY CAUSE © Christian Aid
(2002). Used with permission; extract from the DfES website BULLYING: DON'T SUFFER IN SILENCE – copyright
© DfES; extract from WATERSHIP DOWN by Richard Adams – permission sought; extract from ENCOUNTERS
WITH ANIMALS by Gerald Durrell reproduced with permission of Curtis Brown Ltd, London on behalf of The Estate
of Gerald Durrell. Copyright © The Estate of Gerald Durrell 1958.

First published 2005
Reprinted 2005

Available in the So you really want to learn series:
English, Latin, French, Spanish, Maths, Science

Acknowledgements

This book, like its predecessor, *So You Really Want to Learn English Prep Book 1*, is based on everything I've learned in a long career in English classrooms. And, like all teachers, over the years I've probably learned as much from my pupils about best practice in English lessons as they have learned from me. That learning is in this book. So many thanks go to the hundreds of young people who have passed though my classrooms since 1968.

I also thank, as ever, two Nicholases: Elkin and Oulton. The former is my husband who quietly acts as my backstage researcher, sounding board and 'critical friend'. The latter is my punctilious publisher and editor. Between them, at opposite ends of the process, they 'manage' me.

I am also deeply grateful to Bill Inge, of Ashfold School, Nigel Ramage, of Papplewick School and Geraldine Matthews, of Heath Mount School. Their observation and views have been an invaluable help in the shaping of this book. My thanks also to Jennie Williams of ISEB for her scrupulous eye for detail and for her fantastic support for this project.

Any mistakes which remain are, of course, mine.

Preface

This book is intended for use with 11-13 year olds preparing for Common Entrance. Parts of it could also be useful for younger pupils in need of extension work, or for revision or remedial work with an older group.

Each of the ten chapters is based around three themed extracts: one literary prose, one non-fiction and one poem. The oldest extract is Shakespeare in 1609 and the most recent a news report published in The Daily Telegraph in August 2004. We also wander the world visiting Australia, USA, Thailand, India and Crete as well as popping down to Antarctica with Coleridge. So there's plenty of variety. Each extract is followed by questions designed to encourage close reading and detailed thinking.

Linked to the extracts is a one-year comprehensive English course taking in poetry technique, personal writing, vocabulary, spelling, grammar, punctuation, speaking and listening and wider reading. Each chapter also includes suggestions for extension tasks.

But don't let's allow CE to become the tail that wags the dog. This book is also about helping children to develop a love of reading. I want them to share the pleasures of rigorous, accurate, effective English – not just to pass examinations, but because I believe that the better you are able to communicate in this lovely language of ours, the more fulfilled you are as human being.

S.E. March 2005

Contents

Introduction

Reading Matters

This is a very bookish book. I believe that reading is one of the most essential activities that human beings can undertake. Books do for the mind and soul what food does for the body.

So, almost all the work in this book is based on reading and books. There are questions to encourage you to read closely and carefully. To help you to understand better the tools that poets use in their writing, there is a section on poetry technique in each chapter. Every bit of spelling, vocabulary, grammar and punctuation work is linked to reading. So is much of the speaking and listening. Reading is the backbone of English.

When you are reading a book, it's like a 'direct' phone line between your mind and the author's. You don't need a cast of actors, a TV set, a computer, a teacher, parent or any other assistance. All you need is the printed squiggles on the page and – as if by magic – you're in 'hotline' contact with the mind of, say, Shakespeare who died in 1616 (see Chapter 5) or Dickens (see Chapter 9) who died in 1870. You can share their ideas and stories – instantly. Reading really is remarkable.

That's why every chapter of this book has three separate passages to read and a list of other related reading suggestions under the heading 'Have you read?' I have made these as varied and wide-ranging as I can. I see it as a huge buffet offering you lots of delights – many of them probably unfamiliar to you – to taste.

For example, once you've read the jolly passage from Thomas Hardy's 1872 novel *Under the Greenwood Tree* (Chapter 4) you may decide to buy or borrow the book from the library and read the rest of it. Then, if you like it as much as I do, the good news is that Hardy wrote a number of other novels – and they're all out there waiting for you: *Tess of the D'Urbervilles*, *Far from the Madding Crowd* and *The Woodlanders*, for example. He wrote some fine poetry too.

Or perhaps non-fiction is more to your taste. If Gerald Durrell's often hilarious stories about his life working with animals and in zoos for conservation are new to you, then I hope you are entertained by the passage from *Encounters with Animals* in Chapter 10. If so, I'm sure you'll soon move on to *My Family and Other Animals*, *The Bafut Beagles* and *Three Singles to Adventure*. And there are plenty of other books, fiction and non-fiction, about animals listed in the 'Have You Read?' section of Chapter 10.

This book also contains ten of my favourite poems (plus a couple of spares in the 'And if you've done all that' sections). These are poems that I've shared with many classes. I have found that most pupils, most of the time, like most of them as much as I do. So I hope you enjoy them too. Why not make a collection of your own favourites as you browse in anthologies and other books of poems?

You won't, however, confine yourself to the suggestions made in this book. Reading is a personal adventure, a lifelong, unending treasure hunt. Once you get started, every book you finish opens the door to three (at least!) more. You will be thirsting for more by that author, in that style, on that subject, set in that place or about those characters.

If, for example, you enjoy the *Silas Marner* extract in Chapter 5 and then the rest of the novel, you will probably like other novels by George Eliot such as *The Mill on the Floss*. That could lead you to Charlotte Bronte's *Jane Eyre*, which is also about a woman's struggle against 19th century society. Daphne DuMaurier's *Rebecca* (1938) is similar to *Jane Eyre* and once you've read that you might like other novels by DuMaurier, which might launch you on a quest for more historical fiction (by Philippa Gregory or Rosemary Sutcliff for instance) or novels set in Cornwall . . . and so on and on. Think of it as a journey and go where it takes you.

Or, if you didn't like a particular book, the opposite will be true. You've discovered something about your reading tastes and will change direction on your journey by looking for something different.

English teachers are always telling their pupils that they need to read more. So what exactly will reading do for you?

The more you read:

- the more you know, because every book has a background, setting and incidental factual information which you soak up through reading a story, usually without realising it;

- the more words you will be familiar with, because keen readers learn new vocabulary every day by seeing words in use and recognising their meaning effortlessly;

- the more interesting things you will have to think about and discuss, because books ask questions and suggest ideas;

- the more ideas you will have for your own writing. Remember, all professional writers read a lot;

- the better you will be able to express yourself in writing and speech, because you will be used to seeing (and hearing in your 'mind's ear') good quality English in a wide range of styles.

Convinced?

Good! Then, let's get started.

Chapter 1

Circus

Mark Twain's famous novel **The Adventures of Huckleberry Finn** *was first published in America in 1884. It tells, in his own words, the story of the boy Huck who wants to be free. He runs away from his aunt's farm with the adult black slave, Jim. Together they sail northwards up the Mississippi river. On the way, various things happen, such as seeing a circus.*

1　　It was a real bully circus. It was the splendidest sight that ever was, when they all came riding in, two and two, a gentleman and a lady, side by side, the men just in their drawers and undershorts, and no shoes or stirrups and resting their hands on their thighs, easy and comfortable – there must have been twenty of them – and every lady with a

5　　lovely complexion, and perfectly beautiful, and looking like a gang of real sure-enough queens, and dressed in clothes that cost millions of dollars and just littered with diamonds. It was a powerful first sight. I never see anything so lovely. And then one by one they got up and stood and went a-weaving round the ring so gentle and wavy and graceful, the men looking ever so tall and airy and straight with their heads bobbing and

10　　skimming along, away up there under the tent roof, and every lady's rose-leafy dress flapping soft and silky round her hips and she looking like the loveliest parasol.

And then faster and faster they went, all of them dancing, first one foot stuck out in the air and then the other, the horses leaning more and more and the ringmaster going round and round the centre pole, cracking his whip and shouting 'Hi! Hi! and the clowns

15　　cracking jokes behind them. And by and by all hands dropped the reins and every lady put her knuckles on her hips and every gentleman folded his arms and then how the horses did lean over and hump themselves! And so, one after the other they all skipped off into the ring and made the sweetest bow I ever see and then scampered out, and everybody clapped their hands and went just about wild.

20　　Well, all through the circus they done the most astonishing things and all the time that clown carried on so it most killed the people. The ringmaster couldn't ever say a word to him but he was back at him quick as a wink with the funniest things a body ever said – and how he *could* think of ever so many of them, and so sudden and so pat was what I couldn't noway understand. Why, I couldn't a thought of them in a year. And by and by

25　　a drunk man tried to get into the ring – said he wanted to ride. Said he could ride as well as anybody that ever was. They argued and tried to keep him out but he wouldn't listen and the whole show came to a standstill. Then the people began to holler at him and make fun of him and that made him mad and he began to rip and tear. So that stirred up the people and a lot of men begun to pile down off the benches and swarm towards the

30 ring saying, 'Knock him down! Throw him out!' and one or two women begun to scream. So then the ringmaster he made a little speech and said he hoped there wouldn't be no disturbance. And if the man would promise he wouldn't make no more trouble he would let him ride if he thought he could stay on the horse. So everybody laughed and said all right and the man got on.

35 The minute he was on the horse begun to rip and tear and jump and cavort around with two circus men hanging onto his bridle trying to hold him and the drunk man holding onto his neck and his heels flying in the air at every jump and the whole crowd of people standing up shouting and laughing till the tears rolled down. And at last, sure enough, all the circus men could do, the horse broke loose and away he went like the
40 very nation, round and round the ring with that sot laying down on him and hanging onto his neck with first one leg hanging most to the ground on one side and then t'other one on t'other side and all the people just crazy. It warn't funny to me though. I was all of a tremble to see his danger. But pretty soon he struggled up astraddle and grabbed the bridle, a-reeling his way this and that. And the next minute he dropped the bridle and
45 stood! And the horse going like a house afire too. He just stood there, a-sailing around as easy and comfortable as if he warn't ever drunk in his life – and then he begun to pull off his clothes and sling them. He shed them so thick that they kind of clogged up the air and altogether he shed seventeen suits. And then, there he was, slim and handsome and dressed the gaudiest and the prettiest you ever saw and he lit onto that horse with
50 his whip and made him fairly hum. And finally skipped off and made his bow and danced off to the dressing room and everybody just a-howling with pleasure and astonishment.

Then the ringmaster he see how he had been fooled and he was the sickest ringmaster you ever see, I reckon. Why, it was one of his own men! He had got up that joke all out
55 of his own head and never let on to anybody. Well, I felt sheepish enough to be took in so, but I wouldn't a been in that ringmaster's place, not for a thousand dollars.

(From *The Adventures of Huckleberry Finn* by Mark Twain, 1884)

Exercise 1.1

Now answer these questions as fully as you can. Quote from the passage in your answers.

1. Provide a word or phrase of your own which means the same as the following words as they are used in this passage: (a) bully (line 1), (b) holler (line 27), (c) cavort (line 35), (d) astraddle (line 43), (e) lit (line 49), (f) sheepish (line 55).

2. How would you know from the passage that this story is set in America even if you had not been told?

3. Explain in your own words Huck's initial reaction to the circus.

4. How does Huck feel when he realises the truth about the 'drunk man'?

5. What impression do you get of Huck's character from this passage?

6. What strikes you about Huck's language and why do think Twain makes him speak in this way?

Circus Lion

1   Lumbering haunches, pussyfoot tread, a pride of
        Lions under the arcs
        Walk in, leap up, sit pedestalled there and glum
        As a row of Dickensian clerks

5   Their eyes are slag. Only a muscle flickering
        A bored theatrical roar
        Witness now to the furnaces that drove them
        Exultant along the spoor

        In preyward, elastic leap they are sent through paper
10   Hoops at another's will
        And a whip's crack: afterwards in their cages
        They tear the provided kill.

        Caught young, can this public animal ever dream of
        Stars, distances and thunders?
15   Does he twitch in sleep for ticks, dried water-holes,
        Rogue elephants or hunters?

        Sawdust, not burning desert, is the ground
        Of his to-fro, to-fro pacing,
        Barred with the zebra stripes that imply
20   Sun's free wheel, man's coercing

See this abdicated beast, once king
Of them all, nibble his claws:
Not anger enough left – no, nor despair –
24   To break his teeth on the bars.

(Cecil Day Lewis, 1904-1972)

Poetry technique: Rhythm

Rhythm is the pattern made by an arrangement of short and long sounds. It can be regular and even or irregular and unpredictable. Think of the sound patterns made by a percussion instrument such as a drum in an orchestra or band. Words work like percussion instruments too and all language has rhythm.

When Cecil Day Lewis wrote 'Lumbering haunches, pussyfoot tread' and 'to-fro, to-fro pacing' he was using rhythmic patterns to imitate the movements of the lions.

Look for other interesting examples of rhythm in *Circus Lion* and in the poems used in other chapters of this book.

Exercise 1.2

Now answer these questions on the above poem. Quote the words of the poem in your answers.

1.   Describe in your own words how the lions behave when they first appear.

2.   What is the significance of (a) zebra stripes (line 19), (b) abdicated (line 21).

3.   Why is 'to-fro, to-fro pacing' (line 18) effective?

4.   Choose and comment on three words or phrases which you find interesting and effective.

5.   What do the unanswered questions in the third verse tell you about the poet's attitude to performing animals?

6.   How, by the end of the poem, does the poet imagine that the lions are feeling?

Jumbo-sized protest

1   Animal welfare campaigners have protested at a circus in Trafford with England's only 'performing' elephant.

They asked visitors to boycott last night's Timperley show of the Bobby Roberts Circus – one of just a handful in the country still using performing animals.

5   They were particularly angry about the treatment of Anne, the last remaining circus elephant in the country.

The 51-year-old Asian elephant has been retired from performing, but is paraded during breaks for people to take photographs.

The Manchester Animal Protection Group members arrived at the circus in Green Lane
10   last night to complain at the way Anne and the other animals – eight horses, six ponies and a mule – were kept and transported from town to town.

Elephants are social and intelligent animals who can suffer from physical and mental problems in captivity, say the protesters.

But circus administrator Moira Roberts told the Manchester Evening News: 'The Bobby
15   Roberts Circus has been going for 50 years. Anne, like all the animals, is well-loved and has had excellent care.

'She loves to come into the tent. She has been performing since she was four or five and it would break her heart if we took her away from all the other animals. She's very happy.

'If somebody offered us a million pounds for her we wouldn't take it. She's like one of
20   the family. This is our fifth year in Timperley and we wouldn't keep coming back if they didn't want us.'

The Captive Animals' Protection Society (CAPS) has called on the public to boycott the circus while it is in Timperley – until Sunday – and claims it receives more complaints about it than any other circus.

25   CAPS spokesman Craig Redmond said: 'By their very nature, circuses cannot provide all of the space and necessary requirements to guarantee the well-being of animals. We ask the public to boycott animal circuses and shopkeepers not to display posters for them.'

In December, Anne 'escaped' from the circus at a racecourse in Scotland. But the circus said she merely went 'walkabout' because she was frightened by joy-riders.

30   It is thought no other circus in England features an elephant, though there are some performing elephants at circuses in Northern Ireland.

(John Scheerhout, BBC News, 14th April 2004)

Exercise 1.3

Answer the following questions:

1. Give another word or phrase for (a) paraded (line 7), (b) boycott (line 27).

2. How many animals is the Bobby Roberts Circus using?

3. What is Anne the elephant used for?

4. Why is the word 'escaped' (line 28) in inverted commas?

5. What evidence is there in the passage that Anne does not enjoy her work?

6. Summarise in your own words the arguments against the use of performing animals in circuses. Use only the information provided in the passage.

7. How does the Bobby Roberts Circus justify its use of an elephant? Use your own words.

Exercise 1.4

Your turn to write:

1. Write about a circus or some other sort of live show, play or performance that you have seen.

2. What are your views about performing animals in TV programmes and advertisements and other sorts of production – as well as in circuses?

3. Write a story entitled either 'Circus' or 'Lions'.

4. Imagine you are Anne the elephant and write your story.

5. Write about a circus in any way you wish.

6. Write about a new experience.

Spell check

Although the word 'full' has a double 'l', the related suffix '-ful' in adjectives such as 'beautiful', 'wonderful' and 'powerful' and in nouns such as 'cupful', 'spoonful', 'handful' and 'armful' has only one.

Exercise 1.5

Make a list of as many words ending in '-ful' as you can think of. Arrange them in two columns, one for adjectives and one for nouns.

To form an adverb from adjectives ending in '-ful', add 'ly'. That gives a double 'l'. So:

forget**ful**	forget**fully**
youth**ful**	youth**fully**
use**ful**	use**fully**

Think carefully when you form a plural from a '-ful' noun. It is the main part of the word which takes the 's', not the suffix. So:

one spadeful	three spadesful
one hatful	six hatsful
one teaspoonful	two teaspoonsful

Learn carefully the spellings of these ten words, all of which are taken from the two passages and the poem at the beginning of this chapter:

stirrup	complexion	loveliest	handsome	rogue
campaigners	particularly	necessary	receives	guarantee

Vocabulary

The words 'Dickensian' and 'Boycott' are **eponyms** – names which became words. Behind every eponym there's a story.

Charles Dickens (1812-1870) was an English novelist, author of *Oliver Twist* and *David Copperfield*. The adjective 'Dickensian' describes almost anything Victorian which Dickens features in one of his many books.

Captain Charles Cunningham Boycott (1832-1877) was an Irish estate manager with whom the tenants refused to cooperate because of a dispute about rents. The verb 'to boycott' has come to mean 'to refuse to have dealings with, or buy goods from' a person or organisation.

Exercise 1.6

Match the following ten people's names to the sentences about them:

Charles Macintosh, Dr Rudolph Diesel, Lord Sandwich, Louis Pasteur, Louis Braille, the Duke of Wellington, Alessandro Volta, Monsieur Nicot, Laszlo Biro, Adolphe Sax.

1. He devised a new method of sterilising milk.

2. He invented a new musical instrument.

3. He first introduced tobacco to France.

4. He was a great gambler and, to avoid leaving the gambling tables for a meal, he asked for a slice of meat between two slices of bread.

5. He invented a new type of engine oil, in which ignition of fuel is produced by the heat of air suddenly compressed.

6.   He invented the electric battery and gave his name to a unit of electromotive force.

7.   He wore knee-length rubber boots during military campaigns.

8.   He patented a coat made of waterproof material.

9.   Blinded by a childhood accident, he invented a language of raised dots which is read with the finger tips.

10.   He was a Hungarian journalist who wanted a quick-drying pen, so he invented one with a small steel ball to control the ink flow.

Exercise 1.7

Use a good dictionary or the internet to find out and write notes on the origins of these eponyms:

1.   hoover
2.   morse
3.   lynch
4.   mesmerise
5.   guillotine

6.   bloomers
7.   cardigan
8.   silhouette
9.   jacuzzi
10.   watt

Grammar and punctuation

There are eight **parts of speech** or word classes:

noun	**verb**	**adjective**	**adverb,**
pronoun	**conjunction**	**preposition**	**article**

Every word in any context belongs to one of these eight word classes, most of which will already be familiar to you.

This chapter and the next revise the first six before we move onto the last two which may be new to you.

Nouns

Nouns are naming words. They can be singular or plural. The class includes **proper nouns** (e.g. 'Huck', 'Manchester'), **abstract nouns** (e.g. 'pleasure', 'astonishment') and **collective nouns** (e.g. 'pride' – of lions, or 'pack' – of cards).

Exercise 1.8

Write out these sentences and underline the nouns:

1.   Mark Twain was American.

2.   Lions, tigers and panthers are big cats.

A noun wondering what it means

3. As the Land Rover moved forward with caution, we saw a single elephant and then a whole herd.

4. The circus is coming to town.

5. Anne waved her trunk and then, to our joy, she trumpeted.

6. Hunger was gnawing at me, so I ate some biscuits.

Verbs

Verbs are action or doing words. A verb can consist of several words such as 'will have been eating' or 'is running'. The words 'will have been' and 'is' are **auxiliary** words. These auxiliary words are generally there to show the **tense** of the verb, i.e. **when** the action is happening (past, present or future).

A verb going for a run

Exercise 1.9

Put verbs of your own in the following sentences. Make some of them consist of more than one word.

1. They _____ the public to boycott the circus.

2. All the pupils in this class _____.

3. Afterwards in their cages they _____ the provided kill.

4. I _____ and you _____.

5. Please don't _____.

6. He _____ the bridle and _____.

Adjectives

Adjectives qualify or modify nouns. That means that they change the meaning of the noun or tell you more about it. 'He was a **quiet** man' means something quite different from 'He was a man'.

Mark Twain makes Huck use a lot of adjectives. Reread the passage at the beginning of this chapter. Count the adjectives in the first paragraph and work out why you think there are so many.

Remember that you can never assign words to their word classes unless they are in a context – usually a sentence. This is because words can, and often do, change class according to the job they're doing. It's a bit like your being in one school group, class or set for Maths, but another for French.

For example, consider the words 'break' and 'set':

Try not to **break** that valuable vase. (verb)

I really enjoy **break** buns. (adjective)

Break is my favourite part of the morning. (noun)

An adjective looking rather green

The tennis match had reached **set** point. (adjective)

The gamekeeper **set** the trap to catch a rabbit. (verb)

Freddy is in the top **set** for science. (noun)

Exercise 1.10

Use each of these words in several different sentences of your own so that they belong to different word classes for each use:

part   mean   lift   fast   strip   flower

Exercise 1.11

As you know, every sentence needs to begin with a capital letter and to end with a full stop, question mark or exclamation mark. Punctuate the following sentences correctly:

1.   what a book

2.   one of my favourite authors is Mark Twain

3.   have you read all Cecil Day Lewis's poems

4.   shall I pour the tea

5.   no I won't

6.   it is quite easy to punctuate accurately

Speaking and listening

1.   Work with a partner or in a small group. Practise reading the extract from *The Adventures of Huckleberry Finn* aloud. You will probably find yourselves slipping into a southern American accent – even if you don't try to – because that's the way Twain makes Huck speak.

2.   Learn the poem *Lumbering Haunches* by heart and practise reciting it. Perform it for the rest of the class or to a smaller group.

3.   Prepare a short talk either in favour of performing animals in circuses or against it. There is plenty of information about this on the Internet if you type 'performing animals' into Google or another search engine.

4.   Read one of the books listed in *Have you read?* (on page 13). Tell the class about it.

Have you read?

All of these are stories about circuses, animals or the southern USA (the dates given show when these books were first published):

The Adventures of Huckleberry Finn by Mark Twain (1884)
The Adventures of Tom Sawyer by Mark Twain (1876)
The Road to Memphis by Mildred E Taylor (1990)
The Land by Mildred E Taylor (2003)
Dodgem by Bernard Ashley (1981)
Uncle Tom's Cabin by Harriet Beecher Stowe (1852)
Born Free by Joy Adamson (1960)
Elephant Bill by J H H Williams (1956)
A Trip to the Light Fantastic: Travels with a Mexican Circus by Katie Hickman (1994)
The Complete Poems of C Day Lewis edited by Jill Balcon (1992)

And if you've done all that

- Several states in America have banned the use of *The Adventures of Huckleberry Finn* in schools on the grounds that it is a racist novel. This is mostly because Huck consistently refers to his friend Jim as a 'nigger'. Read the novel very carefully and decide what you think. Work out the reasons for your opinion. *The Day They Came to Arrest the Book* by Nat Hentoff (1985) might help with this. It's a novel about a school from which *Huckleberry Finn* is banned.

- Consider the whole subject of banning books. Is it ever right? If so, for what reasons and who should decide? Read *Fahrenheit 451* by Ray Bradbury (1953) – the title refers to the temperature at which books burn.

- www.theweewebbco.uk/bannedbooks.php lists titles which have been banned somewhere in America. You could use your research as the basis for an article in the school magazine. You might also organise a class or school debate on the subject.

Chapter 2

Survival

An aircraft crash has resulted in a group of schoolboys being stranded without adults on a tropical island.

1   They were on the lip of a cirque[1], or a half-cirque, in the side of a mountain. This was filled with a blue flower, a rock plant of some sort; and the overflow hung down the vent and spilled lavishly among the canopy of the forest. The air was thick with butterflies, lifting, fluttering, settling.

5   Beyond the cirque was the square top of the mountain and soon they were standing on it.

They had guessed before that this was an island: clambering among the pink rocks, with the sea on either side, and the crystal heights of air, they had known by some instinct that the sea lay on every side. But there seemed something more fitting in leaving the last word till they stood on the top, and could see a circular horizon of water.

10   Ralph turned to the others.

'This belongs to us.'

It was roughly boat-shaped: humped near this end with behind them the jumbled descent to the shore. On either side rocks, cliffs, treetops and a steep slope: forward there, the length of the boat, a tamer descent, tree-clad, with hints of pink: and then the jungly flat

15   of the island, dense green, but drawn at the end to a pink tail. There, where the island petered out in water, was another island; a rock, almost detached, standing like a fort, facing them across the green with one bold, pink bastion.

The boys surveyed all this, then looked out to sea. They were high up and the afternoon had advanced; the view was not robbed of sharpness by mirage.

20   'There's a reef. A coral reef. I've seen pictures like that.'

The reef enclosed more than one side of the island, lying perhaps a mile out and parallel to what they now thought of as their beach. The coral was scribbled in the sea as though a giant had bent down to reproduce the shape of the island in a flowing, chalk line but tired before he had finished. Inside was peacock water, rocks and weed showing as in an

25   aquarium; outside was the dark blue of the sea. The tide was running so that long streaks of foam tailed away from the reef and for a moment they felt that the boat was moving steadily astern.

Jack pointed down.

'That's where we landed.'

30 Beyond falls and cliffs, there was a gash visible in the trees; there were the splintered trunks and then the drag, leaving only a fringe of palm between the scar and the sea. There, too, jutting into the lagoon, was the platform with insect-like figures moving near it.

Ralph sketched a twining line from the bald spot on which they stood down a slope, a gully through the flowers, round and down to the rock where the scar started.

35 'That's the quickest way back.'

Eyes shining, mouths open, triumphant, they savoured the right of domination. They were lifted up: were friends.

'There's no village smoke and no boats,' said Ralph wisely. 'We'll make sure later; but I think it's uninhabited.'

40 'We'll get food,' cried Jack. 'Hunt. Catch things . . . until they fetch us.'

Simon looked at them both, saying nothing but nodding till his black hair flopped backwards and forwards: his face was glowing.

Ralph looked down the other way where there was no reef.

'Steeper,' said Jack.

45 Ralph made a cupping gesture.

'That bit of forest down there . . . the mountain holds it up.'

Every coign² of the mountain held up trees – flowers and trees. Now the forest stirred, roared, flailed. The nearer acres of rock flowers fluttered and for half a minute the breeze blew cool on their faces.

50 Ralph spread his arms.

'All ours.'

They laughed and tumbled and shouted on the mountain.

'I'm hungry.'

55 When Simon mentioned his hunger the others became aware of theirs.

'Come on,' said Ralph. 'We've found out what we wanted to know.'

They scrambled down a rock slope, dropped among
60 flowers and made their way under the trees. Here they paused and examined the bushes round them curiously.

Simon spoke first.

'Like candles. Candle bushes. Candle buds.'

65 The bushes were dark evergreen and aromatic and the many buds were waxen green and folded up against the light. Jack slashed at one with his knife and the scent spilled over them.

'Candle buds.'

'You couldn't light them,' said Ralph. 'They just look like candles.'

'Green candles,' said Jack contemptuously. 'We can't eat them. Come on.'

70 They were in the beginnings of the thick forest, plonking with weary feet on a track, when they heard the noises – squeakings – and the hard strike of hoofs on a path. As they pushed forward the squeaking increased till it became a frenzy. They found a piglet caught in a curtain of creepers, throwing itself at the elastic traces in all the madness of extreme terror. Its voice was thin, needle-sharp and insistent. The three boys rushed

75 forward and Jack drew his knife again with a flourish. He raised his arm in the air. There came a pause, a hiatus, the pig continued to scream and the creepers to jerk, and the blade continued to flash at the end of a bony arm. The pause was only long enough for them to understand what an enormity the downward stroke would be. Then the piglet tore loose from the creepers and scurried into the undergrowth. They were left looking

80 at each other and the place of terror. Jack's face was white under the freckles. He noticed that he still held the knife aloft and brought his arm down replacing the blade in the sheath. Then they all three laughed ashamedly and began to climb back to the track.

(From *Lord of the Flies* by William Golding, 1954)

Notes:
[1] rounded hollow
[2] corner

Exercise 2.1

Now answer these questions. Quote from the passage in your answer.

1. Explain the meaning of (a) lavishly (line 3), (b) petered (line 16), (c) bastion (line 17), (d) savoured (line 36), (e) aromatic (line 64), (f) hiatus (line 76).

2. Why do the boys climb to a high point?

3 What is the boys' most urgent practical problem?

4. Which of the boys seems to be emerging as the leader? Give reasons for your answer.

5. What do you learn about Jack's personality from this passage?

6. Summarise the nature of the island and its wildlife. Use your own words.

7. Why do the boys feel ashamed at the end of the passage?

Death of an Aircraft

An incident of the Cretan campaign 1941
To George Psychoundakis

1   One day in our village in the month of July
      An aeroplane sank from the sea of the sky,
          White as a whale it smashed on the shore
          Bleeding oil and petrol all over the floor.

5   The Germans advanced in the vertical heat
      To save the dead plane from the people of Crete
          And round the glass wreck in a circus of snow
          Set seven mechanical sentries to go.

      Seven stalking spiders about the sharp sun
10   Clicking like clockwork and each with a gun
          But at *Come to the Cookhouse* they wheeled about
          And sat down to sausages and sauerkraut.

      Down from the mountain burning so brown
      Wriggled three heroes from Kastelo town,
15   Deep in the sand they silently sank
          And each struck a match for the petrol tank.

      Up went the plane in a feather of fire
      As the bubbling boys began to retire
          And, grey in the guardhouse, seven Berliners
20   Lost their stripes as well as their dinners.

      Down in the village, at murder-stations,
      The Germans fell in friends and relations
          But not a Kastelian snapped an eye
          As he spat in the air and prepared to die.

25   Not a Kastelian whispered a word
      Dressed with the dust to be massacred,
          And squinted up at the sky with a frown
          As three bubbly boys came walking down.

      One was sent to the county gaol,
30   Too young for bullets if not for bail
          But the other two were in prime condition
          To take on a load of ammunition.

      In Archontiki they stood in the weather
      Naked, hungry and chained together:

35   Stark as the stones in the market place
        Under the eyes of the populace.

        Their irons unlocked as their naked hearts
        They faced the squad and their funeral carts,
            The Captain cried, 'Before you're away
40   Is there any last word you'd like to say?'

        'I want no words,' said one 'with my lead,
        Only some water to cool my head.'
            'Water,' the other said, ''s all very fine
            But I'll be taking a glass of wine.'

45   'A glass of wine for the afternoon
        With permission to sing a signature tune!'
            And he ran the raki down his throat
            And took a deep breath for the leading note.

        But before the squad could shoot or say,
50   Like the impala he leapt away
            Over the rifles, under the biers
            The bullets rattling round his ears.

        'Run!' they cried to the boy of stone
        Who now stood there in the street alone,
55   But, 'Rather than bring revenge on your head
            It is better for me to die,' he said.

        The soldiers turned their machine guns round
        And shot him down with a dreadful sound,
            Scrubbed his face with perpetual dark
60   And rubbed it out like a pencil mark.

        But his comrade slept in the olive tree
        And sailed by night on the gnawing sea.
            The soldier's silver shilling earned
            And, armed like an archangel, returned.

(Charles Causley, 1917-2003)

Poetry technique: Metaphor and Simile

Poets (and other writers) continually describe things by comparing them with other things.

Charles Causley's aircraft is 'white as a whale'. This is an example of a **simile**. A simile is a comparison in which the writer uses 'as' or 'like' to spell out what he's doing. Compare 'like a pencil mark' in *Death of an Aircraft* and 'glum as a row of Dickensian clerks' in *Circus Lion* in Chapter 1.

In *Death of an Aircraft* Causley refers to the German guards as 'seven stalking spiders'. This is a shorter, neater sort of comparison and is known as a **metaphor**. He writes as if the guards actually are spiders and expects you to understand what he means.

Sometimes a metaphor can be a single word. Look at 'barred' in *Circus Lion*.

Make a list of similes and metaphors in *Death of an Aircraft* and *Circus Lion*. Work out what each one means and what it adds to the poem.

Together similes and metaphors are known as **imagery** because they create pictures (*images* in French) and work on your *imagination*.

A metaphor stalking a simile

Exercise 2.2

Read *Death of an Aircraft*. Now answer these questions as fully as you can. Try to quote the words of the poem in your responses.

1. Summarise in your own words the story which the poem is telling. Use no more than five sentences.

2. What comparison does the poet use in the first verse to create a picture of the aircraft and its surroundings? How effective do you find it?

3. Explain the meaning of (a) squinted (line 27), (b) signature tune (line 46), (c) perpetual (line 59), (d) gnawing (line 62).

4. 'Too young for bullets if not for bail / But the other two were in prime condition / to take on a load of ammunition.' What is the poet really saying here?

5. Do you think the poem ends in a positive or negative way? Give reasons for your view.

6. What does the rhyme scheme add to the poem?

Villagers plucked from the torrent

In August 2004, the village of Boscastle in Cornwall was seriously flooded.

1   The first indication of the emerging problems in Boscastle was given at 3.46 pm on Monday when a member of the village's cliff rescue team called Falmouth coastguard to say that river levels had risen by 7ft in an hour.

    Ninety minutes later a helicopter pilot reported to the emergency centre at RAF Kinross
5   in north-east Scotland: 'This is a major incident; repeat, major incident. We require all the standby aircraft available. We are in danger of losing the people in the houses.'

For the next three hours there was a continuous shuttle of helicopter rescues that earned the admiration of the 120 people who were plucked to safety from rooftops and trees.

One of the most dramatic rescues was that of 15-month-old Senara Shute.

10 She and her parents, Adrian, 31, and Becky, 22, were saved from the top of their car at Tremaine, seven miles from Boscastle, with Master Aircrewman Clive Chapman, of 203 Squadron at RAF St Mawgan, using the co-pilot's rucksack to hoist the baby into the aircraft.

As the couple risked their lives to try to warn a neighbouring farmer, John Statton, 63,
15 of the danger, he was swept 60ft down the river but managed to cling to a tree.

The baby's mother said: 'Senara was fine. She kept saying "Water, water," and pointing to it and we kept her occupied by getting her to look at the sticks floating past.

'We just made sure we kept calm and kept Senara warm by wrapping Adrian's overalls round her. She hardly cried at all. The rescue man was great, really kind and gentle with
20 her. I think she was interested in what was going on rather than scared.'

Mr Statton said: 'It is a miracle that we are all here. I could have been washed under and their jeep could have been washed away.'

(Michael Fleet, Richard Savill and Ben Fenton in *The Daily Telegraph*, Wednesday 18 August 2004)

Exercise 2.3

Now answer these questions:

1. At what approximate time and date were the rescues completed?

2. Which two things saved Mr Statton's life?

3. What evidence, if any, is there in this passage that the journalists who wrote it were in Cornwall, rather than using telephones from elsewhere to find out what had happened?

4. Summarise everything you learn from this passage about Clive Chapman.

5. What is the significance of the call to Scotland, hundreds of miles from Cornwall?

6. If 120 people were rescued, why do you think the journalists focused on Senara Shute?

Exercise 2.4

Your turn to write:

1. Imagine you are Senara Shute when she has grown up. Tell the story of your dramatic rescue. Your parents will have described it to you many times. Add as much detail as you like.

2. Write a poem about someone surviving under unlikely circumstances. If you wish, you can copy Charles Causley's four-line verse pattern or organise your poem in any other way you like.

3. Imagine a dramatic rescue. Write a newspaper report of it.

4. Write your own desert island story.

5. Why do you think so many stories have been made up and/or told about survival and rescue? Write your views.

6. Write about survival in any way you wish.

Spell check

Words ending in '-e' usually drop the 'e' when 'y' or **suffixes** beginning with a vowel such as '-ed', '-er', or '-ing' are added. So:

stone	stony
enquire	enquiry
combine	combining
suppose	supposing
declare	declaration
spice	spicy

But words ending in '-e' to which a suffix beginning with a consonant is added retain their 'e'. So:

advance	advancement
face	faceless
blame	blameworthy
fire	fireproof
house	household

'Awful' (awe) and 'argument' (argue) are exceptions; learn them!

Exercise 2.5

Add as many suffixes as you can think of to form different, correctly spelled words to the following base words:

1.	mouse		6.	price
2.	lace		7.	shoe
3.	noise		8.	free
4.	bite		9.	service
5.	require		10.	peace

Check that you can spell these ten words from the passages in this chapter:

guessed	descent	parallel	aquarium	flourish
aeroplane	mechanical	wriggled	massacred	continuous

Vocabulary

William Golding uses the geographical term 'cirque' for a feature which is called a 'cwm' in Wales and a 'corrie' in Scotland.

Cirque is a French word which came originally from the Latin word for 'ring': *circus*. We get 'circle', 'circular', 'circuit' and many other words from the same root. A circus was traditionally a performance in a ring and at Piccadilly Circus, for example, the traffic makes a ring round a central point (the statue of Eros, in the case of Piccadilly Circus).

The Latin word *circum*, which stems from *circus*, is also used as a prefix. It means 'around' and various English words derive from it.

Exercise 2.6

Put the correct words beginning with 'circum-' into these sentences. The words you need are listed at the end.

1. One of the boys in Charles Causley's poem managed to _____ the German occupation.

2. When we practise speaking and listening, we are always advised to avoid _____ and to be very direct.

3. The outer edge of any circle is known as the _____.

4. The _____ Leeds Castle in Kent is a popular tourist attraction because people love buildings on islands.

5. I like to read the _____ on my grandfather's medals.

6. My elder brother keeps his thoughts well reined in but my younger brother is much less _____.

circumscription	circumvent	circumfluous
circumference	circumspect	circumlocution

Exercise 2.7

A 'Berliner' is someone who lives in Berlin. A 'Venetian' is an inhabitant of Venice.

Words like 'Berliner' and 'Venetian' are **toponyms**, from the Greek *topos*, meaning 'place'.

Where do people with the following toponyms come from?

1. Mancunian
2. Parisian
3. Londoner
4. Neopolitan
5. Liverpudlian
6. Sicilian
7. Oxonian
8. Hamburger
9. Glaswegian
10. Florentine

Exercise 2.8

Mr and Mrs Shute kept Senara warm by wrapping her in her father's 'overalls'. Use the following words in sentences of your own to show that you understand their meaning:

1. overreact
2. overburden
3. overdress
4. overfamiliar
5. overcast
6. overdraw
7. overlap
8. overhear
9. overcome
10. overlook

Grammar and punctuation

Adjectives

An **adjective** qualifies or modifies a noun. It adds to its meaning or tells you more about it:

> **cupping** gesture
> **many** buds
> **deep** breath
> **dreadful** sound
> **helicopter** pilot

It doesn't necessarily go next to the noun it qualifies:

> The rescue man was **great**.
> They stood in the weather/ **Naked**, **hungry**.
> Its voice was **thin**, **needle-sharp**, **insistent**.

An adjective looking rather red

Exercise 2.9

Write out the following sentences. Underline the adjectives. Draw a line linking them to the nouns they qualify.

1. Ralph sketched a twining line from the bald spot.

2. Simon's face was red.

3. And, grey in the guardhouse, seven Berliners / Lost their stripes as well as their dinners.

4. The rescue of Senara Shute was dramatic.

5. Well-respected and admired, Charles Causley was a fine poet.

6. They ran, thin and eager, along the shore.

Adverbs

Adverbs qualify or modify verbs:

> They **silently** sank.
> All three laughed **ashamedly**.
> She **kept** saying
> She **hardly** cried.

Or sometimes they modify other adverbs or adjectives:

> **very** quickly
> **happily** married

An adverb qualifying a verb

They tell you how or when something is done or happens.

Occasionally an **adverb** modifies a whole sentence:

> **Unfortunately**, it's raining today.
> We learned, **however**, that games had been cancelled.

Exercise 2.10

Write out the following sentences underlining the adverbs:

1. Sadly, there will not be time to visit this museum.

2. We said we were extremely sorry and left.

3. Are you still hungry?

4. We need to get this work done fast.

5. Dismally and reluctantly, they packed up their tent.

6. Jabinda moved forwards while Fred slid backwards, but both should have been going clockwise.

Commas

Remember that a sentence begins with a **capital** letter and ends with a **full stop**, **exclamation** or **question mark**. Think of it as a closed box.

Inside the box you may – or may not – need **commas** for various reasons.

For example, commas can be used to separate the name of the person being spoken to from the rest of the sentence:

> 'Oliver, please put the chairs straight.'

> 'What do you think, Emma?'

> 'Did you know, Mum, that I had made the supper?'

Or you can use them to divide the items in a list – which can be nouns, adjectives, adverbs or verbs – but not before the final 'and':

> I bought oranges, bananas, apples, peaches and plums.

> The children ran, skipped, hopped, jumped and thoroughly enjoyed themselves.

> My father came in with a delightful, tiny, wriggling, brown puppy.

> We did it happily, willingly, knowingly and fast.

Exercise 2.11

Discuss with a partner where the commas should go in the following examples. Be sure that you know exactly why you need a comma where you do.

1. 'Peter please bring me the paper glue stapler and pens.'

2. 'Did you see that enormous slinky black cat?'

3. 'What an amazing story Jake!'

4. We heard Perry playing singing and tuning his violin while his twin sister Abigail was outside trampolining catching throwing and exercising.

5. 'Everybody will you listen please!'

6. Maria's Tuesday lessons included Maths PE Geography English and French.

7. 'Sit down Melissa and I'll explain.'

Speaking and listening

1. Interview someone who has survived something. Many older people remember the bombing of London and other cities in the 1940s, for example. Or you may know someone who has survived a serious accident or illness. Ask them who, what, when, why and how questions.

2. Work with a partner. Imagine that one of you has been in a very dangerous situation and the other is the rescuer. Work out the exact circumstances and what you would say to each other.

3. Work in a group of five or six. Choose a role each – probably someone famous or important. Imagine you are in a hot air balloon which is losing height. The only way the balloon will stay in the air is if weight is shed and that means one of the occupants must be thrown out. Take turns to persuade the group that you – in your role – should not be the one. Once you've had a bit of practice at this, you and your teacher might be able to organise a whole class balloon debate.

4. Prepare a short talk called 'How to Survive'. Interpret this in any way you like (it need not be serious). Give your talk to the rest of the class.

Have you read?

All of these are stories about survival at various points in history and the future:

Lord of the Flies by William Golding (1954)
Robinson Crusoe by Daniel Defoe (1719)
The Odyssey by Homer (c. 8th century B.C.)
Parcel of Patterns by Jill Paton Walsh (1983)
Plague 99 by Jean Ure (1989)
Death of Grass by John Christopher (1956)
Z for Zachariah by Robert O'Brien (1975)
The Chrysalids by John Wyndham (1955)
Kensuke's Kingdom by Michael Morpurgo (1999)
Brother in the Land by Robert Swindells (1984)

And if you've done all that

- Read Shakespeare's play *The Tempest*, really an early example of a shipwreck survival story. Try also to see a production or watch a video of the play. Make an informative wall poster based on it for the classroom wall.

- Each of these was a famous disaster from which only a handful of people survived: the eruption of Vesuvius in AD 79; the Massacre at Cawnpore in India in 1857; the sinking of the Titanic in 1912. Find out as much as you can about one or more of them, using the Internet or reference books or both. Prepare a short presentation on your chosen topic(s) for the rest of the class or for a school assembly.

Chapter 3

Race

Sephy is a 'cross', a black girl, and her friend Callum is a 'nought' and white. In the world created by Malorie Blackman in this novel, crosses are superior and have all the advantages in society, although the two groups now attend the same schools and are, in theory, equal.

1   I lined up in the food queue. I wasn't going to do anything out of the ordinary, so why was my heart bumping in such a strange way? I collected my chicken and mushroom pie with the usual over-boiled trimmings, my jam tart with over-sweet custard and my carton of milk and, taking a deep breath, I headed for Callum's table. Callum and the other

5   noughts glanced up as I approached their table, only to look away again immediately.

'D'you mind if I join you?'

They all looked so shocked, it wasn't even funny. The other noughts continued to look stunned, but Callum's expression turned. I sat down before he could say no and before I could bottle out.

10   'What d'you think you're doing?' he snapped.

'Eating my lunch,' I replied before cutting into my pie. I tried to smile at the other three noughts but they instantly returned to eating their food.

'Hi. I'm Sephy Hadley.' I thrust my hand under the nose of the nought girl I was sitting next to. She had a dark brown plaster on her forehead which stuck out on her pale white

15   skin like a throbbing thumb. 'Welcome to Heathcroft.'

She looked at my hand like it was about to bite her. Wiping her own hand on her tunic, she then took mine and shook it slowly.

'I'm Shania,' she said softly.

'That's a pretty name. What does it mean?' I asked.

20   Shania shrugged. 'It doesn't mean anything.'

'My mother told me my name means "serene night",' I laughed. 'But Callum will tell you I'm anything but serene!'

Shania smiled at me. It was tentative and brief but at least it was genuine – while it lasted.

'How's your head?' I asked, pointing at the plaster.

25   'It's OK. It'll take more than a stone step to dent my head.'

I smiled. 'That plaster's a bit noticeable.'

'They don't sell pink plasters. Only dark brown ones.' Shania shrugged.

My eyes widened at that. I'd never really thought about it before, but she was right. I'd never seen any pink plasters. Plasters were the colour of us crosses, not the noughts.

30   'Sephy, just what d'you think you're doing?' Mrs Bawden, the deputy headmistress, appeared from nowhere to scowl down at me.

'Pardon?'

'What're you doing?'

'I'm eating my lunch.' I frowned.

35   'Don't be facetious.'

'I'm not. I'm eating my lunch.'

'Get back to your own table – at once.' Mrs Bawden looked like she was about to erupt kittens.

I looked around. I was now the centre of attention – the very last thing I'd wanted.

40   'B-but I'm sitting h-here,' I stammered.

'Get back to your own table – NOW!'

What table? I didn't have my own table. And then it dawned on me exactly what Mrs Bawden meant. She wasn't talking about me getting back to my own table. She was talking about me getting back to my own kind. I glanced around. Callum and the others
45   weren't looking at me. Everyone else was. They weren't.

'I'm sitting with my friend, Callum,' I whispered. I could hardly hear my own voice so I have no idea how Mrs Bawden heard me – but she did. She grabbed my arm and pulled me out of my chair. I was still holding on to my tray, and everything on it went flying.

50 'Persephone Hadley, you will come with me.' Mrs Bawden yanked me away from the table and dragged me across the food hall. I tried to twist away from her, but she had a grip like a python on steroids. I turned my head this way and that. Wasn't anyone going to do anything? Not from the look of it. I twisted sharply to look at Callum. He was watching but the moment I caught his eye, he looked away. I stopped struggling after that. I straightened up and followed Mrs Bawden to the headmaster's office.

55 Callum had turned away from me. I didn't care about the rest but I cared about that. He'd turned away . . . . Well, I was slow getting the message, but I'd finally got it. God knows, I'd finally got it.

*　　*　　*

Callum

I had to get out of there. I left my lunch half-eaten and walked out of the food hall
60 without saying a word to any of the others.

I had to get out of there.

I walked out of the food hall and out of the building and out of the school, my steps growing ever faster and more frantic – until by the time I was out of the school gates, I was running. Running until my back ached and my feet hurt and my heart was ready to
65 burst and still I kept running. I ran all the way out of the town and down to the beach. I collapsed onto the cool sand, my body bathed in sweat. I lay on my stomach and punched the sand. And again, and again. Until my knuckles were red raw and bleeding.

(From *Noughts and Crosses* by Malorie Blackman, 2001)

Exercise 3.1

Answer these questions. Quote from the passage in your answers.

1. Explain the meaning of (a) tentative (line 23), (b) facetious (line 35), (c) erupt (line 37).

2. Why does Sephy sit with Callum and his nought friends?

3. Why do you think Malorie Blackman makes Sephy tell you in detail what food she has on her tray?

4. Explain the significance of Shania's sticking plaster.

5. Comment on the comparisons 'like a throbbing thumb' (line 15) and 'like a python on steroids' (line 51). What do they show you about Sephy's character?

6. What is the 'message' which Sephy eventually 'gets' (lines 56 and 57)?

7. Why do you think Callum reacts as he does? What is he feeling?

Telephone Conversation

1   The price seemed reasonable, location
     Indifferent. The landlady swore she lived
     Off premises. Nothing remained
     But self-confession. 'Madam,' I warned,
5   'I hate a wasted journey – I am African.'
     Silence. Silenced transmission of
     Pressurised good-breeding. Voice, when it came,
     Lipstick coated, long gold-rolled
     Cigarette-holder pipped. Caught I was, foully.
10   'HOW DARK?' . . . I had not misheard . . . 'ARE YOU LIGHT
     OR VERY DARK?' Button B. Button A[1]. Stench
     Of rancid breath of public hide-and-speak.
     Red booth. Red pillar-box. Red double-tiered
     Omnibus squelching tar. It *was* real! Shamed
15   By ill-mannered silence, surrender
     Pushed dumbfounded to beg simplification.
     Considerate she was, varying the emphasis –
     'ARE YOU DARK? OR VERY LIGHT?' Revelation came.
     'You mean – like plain or milk chocolate?'
20   Her assent was clinical, crushing in its light
     Impersonality. Rapidly, wave-length adjusted,
     I chose. 'West African sepia[2].' and as afterthought,
     'Down in my passport.' Silence for spectroscopic
     Flight of fancy, till truthfulness clanged her accent
25   Hard on the mouthpiece. 'WHAT'S THAT?' conceding
     'DON'T KNOW WHAT THAT IS.' 'Like brunette.'
     'THAT'S DARK, ISN'T IT?' 'Not altogether.
     Facially, I am brunette, but, madam, you should see
     The rest of me. Palm of my hand, soles of my feet
30   Are a peroxide[3] blond. Friction, caused –
     Foolishly, madam – by sitting down, has turned
     My bottom raven black – One moment, madam! – sensing
     Her receiver rearing on the thunderclap
     About my ears – 'Madam,' I pleaded, 'wouldn't you rather
35   See for yourself?'

(Wole Soyinka, born 1934)

Notes:

[1] buttons A and B were part of the telephone system in call boxes before the introduction of
   automatic connection

[2] pale brown dye extracted from cuttle fish and used to tint old photographs

[3] chemical used to turn dark hair light

Poetry technique: Irony

Irony is the humorous or mildly sarcastic use of words to mean the opposite of what they normally mean.

Look at 'nothing remained / But self-confession' and 'Considerate she was' in *Telephone Conversation* for example.

Compare these lines from *Death of an Aircraft*:

> Too young for bullets if not for bail
> But the other two were in prime condition
> To take in a load of ammunition.

What is Causley's point? Practise expressing his view in your own words without the use of irony.

Exercise 3.2

Read the poem *Telephone Conversation* and then answer these questions as fully as you can. Quote from the poem in your answers.

1. Why does the narrator 'confess' to the woman that he is African (line 5)?

2. In what way does her reaction surprise him?

3. Explain the meaning of (a) pressurised (line 7), (b) rancid (line 12), (c) assent (line 20).

4. What evidence is there in the poem to show that this conversation took place in the 1950s or 1960s?

5. List all the words or phrases which describe colour in the poem.

6. What do you deduce from the poem about the educational background of (a) the narrator and (b) the woman? Give reasons.

7. Why does he mention his bottom?

8. What features make *Telephone Conversation* a poem rather than a story?

I have a dream

Doctor Martin Luther King was a black American clergyman who led a massive campaign for equal rights for black people, especially in the southern states of the US. This extract is from a famous speech he made in 1963 in Washington DC. Five years later he was assassinated in Memphis, Tennessee.

1   I am not unmindful that some of you have come here out of great trials and tribulations. Some of you have come fresh from narrow jail cells. Some of you have come from areas where your quest for freedom left you battered by the storms of persecution and staggered by the winds of police brutality. You have been the veterans of creative
5   suffering. Continue to work with the faith that unearned suffering is redemptive.

Go back to Mississippi, go back to Alabama, go back to South Carolina, go back to Georgia, go back to Louisiana, go back to the slums and ghettoes of our northern cities, knowing that somehow this situation can and will be changed. Let us not wallow in the valley of despair.

10   I say to you today, my friends, that in spite of the difficulties and frustrations of the moment I still have a dream. It is a dream deeply rooted in the American dream.

I have a dream that one day this nation will rise up and live out the true meaning of its creed: 'We hold these truths to be self-evident; that all men are created equal.'

I have a dream that one day on the red hills of Georgia the sons of former slaves and the
15   sons of former slave owners will be able to sit down together at the table of brotherhood.

I have a dream that one day even in the state of Mississippi, a desert state sweltering with the heat of injustice and oppression, will be transformed into an oasis of freedom and justice.

20   I have a dream that my four little children will one day live in a nation where they will not be judged by the colour of their skin but by the content of their character.

I have a dream today.

I have a dream that one day every valley shall be exalted, every hill and mountain shall be made low, the rough places will be made plains and the crooked places will be made
25   straight, and the glory of the Lord shall be revealed, and all flesh shall see it together.

This is our hope. This is the faith with which I return to the south. With this faith we will be able to hew out of the mountain of despair a stone of hope. With this faith we will be able to transform the jangling discords of our nation into a beautiful symphony of brotherhood. With this faith we will be able to work together, to pray together, to
30   struggle together, to go to jail together, to stand up for freedom together, knowing that we will be free one day.

(Martin Luther King, from a speech made on 28th August, 1963)

Exercise 3.3

Answer these questions. Refer closely to the passage in your answers.

1. In which American state did black people have the hardest time, according to Martin Luther King?

2. Explain the meaning of (a) veterans (line 4), (b) ghettoes (line 7), (c) creed (line 13), (d) exalted (line 23).

3. Sum up Dr King's hopes for the future in not more than two sentences.

4. What do you think Dr King means by (a) 'unearned suffering is redemptive' (line 5), (b) 'a beautiful symphony of brotherhood' (lines 28-29)?

5. If you hadn't been told that Dr King was a clergyman how could you tell from (a) what he says and (b) the way he says it?

6. In what ways does the style of this speech – meant to be heard – differ from a persuasive opinion written to be read silently in, for example, a newspaper?

7. Why does Dr King repeat himself so often? Do you find it effective?

Exercise 3.4

Your turn to write:

1 Sephy and Callum in *Noughts and Crosses* are very close friends. Imagine the next time they meet privately and describe what happens and what they say to each other.

2. Imagine you are the woman phoned by the narrator of Wole Soyinka's poem. Write your version of what happened as if you were writing a letter to a friend. Develop her personality in any way you wish.

3. Write about race in any way you wish.

4. Write a poem or story of your own entitled 'Telephone Call'.

5. Write a persuasive speech on any subject you wish. Use some of the methods used by Martin Luther King and remember that a good speech is very different in style and tone from an essay.

6. Write a story called 'A Stone of Hope'.

Spell check

To form the plural of nouns which end with '-y' we usually change the 'y' to 'ies' when the letter before the 'y' is a **consonant**. So:

opportunity	opportunities
baby	babies
nursery	nurseries
jelly	jellies

With nouns which have a **vowel** before the 'y' we simply add 's' in the plural. So:

monkey	monkeys
boy	boys
quay	quays

An exception to this is 'money' whose plural is 'monies' – a technical term generally used only in banking.

Exercise 3.5

Write the correctly spelled plurals of the following words:

laboratory	lady	fly	buoy	kidney
alloy	apology	entry	Monday	symphony

Check that you can spell these ten words taken from the three passages above:

immediately	collapsed	stomach	premises	surrender
emphasis	chocolate	adjusted	conceding	receiver

What do you notice about the spelling of 'facetious'? This is very unusual in English.

Vocabulary

'Spectroscopic', which originally referred to a scientific instrument the spectroscope, means 'visually wide ranging'. It was formed in the nineteenth century from the Latin word *spectrum* ('something seen') and the Greek word *scopeo* ('to look at').

Exercise 3.6

What do these words mean? Try to work them out for yourself if they're new to you. Then use a dictionary to check.

1. scope
2. telescope
3. microscope
4. kaleidoscope
5. periscope
6. stethoscope
7. spectrum
8. spectral
9. spectacle
10. spectate

Exercise 3.7

'Redemptive' is the adjective formed from the verb 'to redeem' and the linked noun 'redemption'.

Use the following forms of words, which may not be familiar to you, in sentences of your own, to show that you understand their meaning:

1. discursive (adjective from the verb 'to discuss' and the noun 'discussion')

2. condemnation (noun from the verb 'to condemn')

3.   illustrative (adjective from the verb 'to illustrate' and the noun 'illustration')

4.   illusory (adjective from the noun 'illusion')

5.   opportune (adjective from the noun 'opportunity')

6.   severity (noun from the adjective 'severe')

7.   adjectival (adjective from the noun 'adjective')

8.   quantify (verb from the noun 'quantity')

9.   opine (verb from the noun 'opinion')

10.   ascertain (verb from the adjective 'certain')

Grammar and punctuation

Conjunctions

Conjunctions are joining words. (Remember that a junction on a railway line is a joining place.)

They can join two or more short sentences together to make one (differently punctuated) longer sentence or they can join ideas or words within a sentence.

because	although	whereas	since	and
but	as	while	or	until
despite	however	after	before	yet
though	notwithstanding	nonetheless		

can all be used as conjunctions. Add to this list yourself. Watch for them in your reading and make yourself aware of how they work.

Try to use conjunctions imaginatively in your writing. You don't always have to use the most obvious one.

Exercise 3.8

Write out the following sentences putting conjunctions in the spaces:

1.   Martin Luther King was an impressive speaker _____ not everyone liked what he said.

2.   Wole Soyinka, a fine poet _____ playwright, _____ won the Nobel prize for Literature in 1986.

3.   _____ her good intentions Sephy Hadley showed Callum up in a public place.

4.   _____ I have finished *Noughts and Crosses* I want to read the sequel *Knife Edge*.

5.   Malorie Blackman wrote *Noughts and Crosses* _____ Beverley Naidoo wrote *Out of Bounds*.

6.   Did you enjoy Wole Soyinka's poem _____ perhaps you prefer something more traditional?

Pronouns

A **pronoun** is a word which stands in place of a noun. There are various sorts of pronoun. Here are two which may be new to you:

A **demonstrative pronoun** is one which indicates (or demonstrates) precisely which one of something is meant. Think of it as being accompanied by a gesture. There are four in Standard English:

> **this**　　　**these**　　　**that**　　　**those**

(You might hear or read others such as *yon* or *yonder* in Scotland.)

> I like **this**.
> **These** are my favourites.
> **That** is the best.
> **Those** are worst.

Alternatively, they can be used, like adjectives, in front of nouns to modify them.

> **This** book is brilliant.
> **Those** plums are sour.
> Did you see **that** car?
> Put **these** papers away.

A **relative pronoun** is one which introduces a subordinate clause in a sentence and refers to a noun which has gone before it in the sentence. **Who**, **whom**, **which** and **that** are the commonest.

> This is the boy **who** is coming to supper tomorrow.

('who is coming to supper tomorrow' is a subordinate clause and 'who' points back to the noun 'boy')

> Wole Soyinka comes from Nigeria, **which** is in West Africa

('which is in West Africa' is a subordinate clause and 'which' looks back to 'Nigeria')

> My uncle, to **whom** I owe a great deal, has died.

('to whom I owe a great deal' is a subordinate clause and 'whom' refers to 'uncle'.)

If you learn Latin, you will know (I'm sure) to use 'whom' with the accusative, genitive, dative and ablative cases. If not, remember to use 'whom' when you would otherwise say 'him'. The '-m' at the end of both words is significant.

> My uncle has died. I owe a lot to **him**.

And use 'whom' after the prepositions 'by', 'with' or 'from':

> My granny, from **whom** I learned to cook, lives in Somerset.

> Martin Luther King lived with his wife, by **whom** he had four children.

> Sephy Hadley admired Callum, with **whom** she tried to share a table.

The noun in the sentence to which the relative pronoun refers in all these examples is called, in grammar, the **antecedent**.

Exercise 3.9

Put demonstrative or relative pronouns in the spaces in these sentences. Write in brackets after each sentence which sort of pronoun(s) you have used.

1. My brother, ____ hates cabbage, actually ate some when he was away at camp.

2. Shall I put the books on ____ shelf or on ____ one?

3. ____ is my pen.

4. I like ____ dress.

5. We still have all the glasses ____ my parents were given as a wedding present.

6. Wole Soyinka, to ____ many fine tributes have been written, was 70 in 2004.

7. My aunt, with ____ my uncle raised a large family, is a wonderful mother.

8. We seem to have hotter summers ____ days.

Exercise 3.10

More practice with commas

Remember that a sentence is a closed box starting with a **capital letter** and ending with a **full stop**, **question mark**, or **exclamation mark**. Commas can be used only inside the box (see Chapter 2). Commas are often a matter of choice and taste. Many commas are optional. The general trend now is to use fewer commas rather than more, but sometimes they are necessary to mark a pause within a sentence and to make the meaning clear.

Add commas to these sentences:

1. If it is fine tomorrow I should like to play cricket.

2. Although I have read many of Wole Soyinka's poems I have yet to see any of his plays.

3. When I saw how tired she looked I decided not to tell her of our plans but she asked me about them saying how interested she was so I had no choice.

4. In May this year Emma Courtenay joined our school as a member of Year 7 and as she loves maths she is actively looking for ways of doing more getting really good marks and taking GCSE early.

5. Meanwhile Mrs Bawden had crept up on Sephy silent and determined.

6. Shall we pack up now carry on for a bit longer take a break or get ourselves a drink of tea coffee or juice to sip while we're working?

Speaking and listening

1. Work with a partner on Wole Soyninka's *Telephone Call*. One of you should read the narrator's part and the other the woman's. When you're satisfied with your work, join up with another pair and listen to each other's interpretation.

2. Working in a pair, develop a telephone conversation in which the speakers are disagreeing or misunderstand each other. Choose any subject you wish.

3. Read Martin Luther King's speech aloud several times to feel its rhythms. What do you notice about the speed at which you have to take it? Work out why this is.

4. Work in a group of four. Discuss why you think there is so much racial tension in different parts of the world. What could be done to make things better? When you've finished your discussion, a spokesperson for your group should summarise your group's views for the rest of the class.

5. Read one of the books in *Have you read?* Tell the rest of the class about it.

Have you read?

All these books have racial themes:

Noughts and Crosses by Malorie Blackman (2001)
Knife Edge by Malorie Blackman (2004)
Out of Bounds by Beverley Naidoo (2001)
The Joy Luck Club by Amy Tan (1989)
Things Fall Apart by Chinua Achebe (1958)
One More River by Lynne Reid Banks (1973)
The Road to Memphis by Mildred E Taylor (1990)
Across the Barricades by Joan Lingard (1972)
To Kill a Mockingbird by Harper Lee (1960)
Cry the Beloved Country by Alan Paton (1948)
To Sir With Love by ER Braithwaite (1959)
A Wedding Man is Nicer Than Cats Miss by Rachel Scott (1971)

And if you've done all that

●   Find out what you can about the American Civil Rights movement in the 1960s from books and the Internet. Develop your findings into a short presentation for the rest of the class.

●   Benjamin Zephaniah and Grace Nicholls are well-known British black poets. Read some of their poems and create your own anthology of your favourites.

●   Work with a partner. Write a short play in which race is a theme. Newspapers can be useful sources of story ideas.

Chapter 4

Carol singers

It is Christmas Eve in the early nineteenth century in the village of Mellstock (loosely based on the Dorset villages of Stinsford and Lower Bockhampton). Carol singers, and the traditional musicians who accompanied hymns in church before organs were usual, known collectively as 'the choir', are doing their annual rounds.

1   An increasing light made itself visible in one of the windows of the upper floor. It came so close to the blind that the exact position of the flame could be perceived from the outside. Remaining steady for an instant the blind went upward from before it, revealing to thirty concentrated eyes a young girl framed as a picture by the window architrave and
5   unconsciously illuminating her countenance to a vivid brightness by a candle she held in her left hand, close to her face. She was wrapped in a white robe of some kind, whilst down her shoulders fell a twining profusion of marvellously rich hair, in a wild disorder which proclaimed it to be only during the night that such a condition was discoverable. Her bright eyes were looking into the gray world outside with an uncertain expression,
10   oscillating between courage and shyness which, as she recognised the semicircular group of dark forms gathered before her, transformed itself into pleasant resolution.

Opening the window, she said lightly and warmly:

'Thank you singers, thank you!'

Together went the window quickly and quietly and the blind started downward on its
15   return to its place. Her fair forehead and eyes vanished; her little mouth; her neck and shoulders; all of her. Then the spot of candlelight shone nebulously as before; then it moved away.

'How pretty!' exclaimed Dick Dewy.

'If she'd been rale waxwork she couldn't ha been comelier,' said Michael Mail.

20   'As near a thing to a spiritual vision as ever I wish to see,' said tranter[1] Dewy fervently.

All the rest, after clearing their throats and adjusting their hats, agreed that such a sight was worth singing for.

'Now to Farmer Shinar's, and then replenish our insides, Father,' said the tranter.

'Wi' all my heart,' said old William, shouldering his bass-viol[2].

25   Farmer Shinar's was a queer lump of a house, standing at the corner of a lane that ran obliquely into the principal thoroughfare. The upper windows were much wider than

they were high, and this feature, together with a broad bay window where the door might have been expected, gave it by day the aspect of a human countenance turned askance, and wearing a sly and wicked leer.

30   'Forty breaths and number thirty two – "Behold the morning star"!' said old William.

They had reached the end of the second verse and the fiddlers were doing the up stroke previously to pouring forth the opening chord of the third verse, when, without a light appearing or any signal being given, a roaring voice exclaimed:

'Shut up! Don't make your blaring row here. A feller wi' a headache enough to split
35   likes a quiet night.'

Slam went the window.

'Hullo, that's an ugly blow for we artists!' said the tranter, in a keenly appreciative voice and turning to his companions.

'Finish the carrel, all who be friends of harmony!' said old William commandingly: and
40   they continued to the end.

'Forty breaths and number nineteen!' said William firmly. 'Give it to him well; the choir can't be insulted in this manner!'

A light now flashed into existence, the window opened, and the farmer stood revealed as one in a terrific passion.

45   'Drown en! – drown en!' the tranter cried, fiddling frantically. 'Play fortissmy and drown his spaking!'

'Fortissmy!' said Michael Mail, and the music and singing waxed so loud that it was impossible to know what Mr Shinar had said, was saying or was about to say: but wildly flinging his arms and body about in the form of capital Xs and Ys, he appeared to utter
50   enough invectives to consign the whole parish to perdition.

'Very unseemly – very!' said old William, as they retired. 'Never such a dreadful scene in the whole round o' my carrel practice – never!'

They now crossed the Twenty-Acres to proceed to the lower village, and met Voss with the hot mead and bread and cheese as they were crossing the churchyard. This
55   determined them to eat and drink before proceeding further, and they entered the belfry[3]. The lanterns were opened and the whole body sat round against the walls on benches and whatever else was available and made a hearty meal. In the pauses of conversation could be heard throughout the floor overhead a little world of undertones and creaks from the halting clockwork which never spread further than the tower they were born in.

60   Having done eating and drinking, the instruments were again tuned, and once more the party emerged into the night air.

'Where's Dick?' said old Dewy.

Every man looked round him upon every other man as if Dick might have been transmuted into one or the other: and then they said that they didn't know.

65 'He've clinked off home-along, depend upon't!' suggested one of the men.

'I hope no fatal tragedy has overtook the lad!' said his grandfather.

'O no,' replied tranter Dewy placidly. 'Wonder where he've put that there fiddle of his. Why that fiddle cost thirty shillens, and good words besides. Somewhere in the damp, without doubt; that there instrument will be unglued and spoilt in ten minutes.'

70 'What in the name o' righteousness can have happened?' said old William still more uneasily.

(Adapted from *Under the Greenwood Tree* by Thomas Hardy, 1872)

Notes:
[1] someone who earned his living as a casual delivery man
[2] an old stringed instrument played wedged upright on the lap like a small 'cello
[3] church tower with bells

Exercise 4.1

Answer the following questions as fully as you can. Quote from the passage in your answers.

1. Explain the meaning of (a) oscillating (line 10), (b) nebulously (line 16), (c) transmuted (line 64).

2. Find expressions in the passage which mean exactly the same as (a) eat a good meal, (b) to be swearing strongly, (c) joined the main road at an angle.

3. How many men were there in the choir?

4. Explain why the girl's hair was particularly fascinating.

5. Thomas Hardy was an architect by training. Which details in the passage show his interest?

6. Explain why William insists that the choir sing and play on outside Farmer Shinar's house.

7. What do you think has happened to Dick?

8. Thomas Hardy was an amateur violinist. How might you have guessed that from this passage?

Christmas

1   The bells of waiting Advent ring,
         The Tortoise stove is lit again
     And lamp-oil light across the night
         Has caught the streaks of winter rain
5   In many a stained-glass window sheen
     From Crimson Lake to Hooker's Green.

     The holly in the windy hedge
         And round the Manor House the yew
     Will soon be stripped to deck the ledge,
10   The altar, font and arch and pew,
     So that the villagers can say
     'The church looks nice' on Christmas Day.

     Provincial public-houses blaze
         And Corporation tramcars clang,
15   On lighted tenements I gaze
         Where paper decorations hang,
     And bunting in the red Town Hall
     Says 'Merry Christmas to you all'.

     And London shops on Christmas Eve
20   Are strung with silver bells and flowers
     As hurrying clerks the city leave
         To pigeon-haunted classic towers,
     And marbled clouds go scudding by
     The many-steepled London sky.

25   And girls in slacks remember Dad,
         And oafish louts remember Mum,
     And sleepless children's hearts are glad,
         And Christmas-morning bells say 'Come!'
     Even to shining ones who dwell
30   Safe in the Dorchester Hotel.

     And is it true? And is it true,
         This most tremendous tale of all,
     Seen in a stained glass window's hue,
         A Baby in an ox's stall?
35   The Maker of the stars and sea
     Became a Child on earth for me?

     And is it true? For if it is,
         No loving fingers tying strings

Around those tissued fripperies,
40   The sweet and silly Christmas things,
Bath salts and inexpensive scent
And hideous tie so kindly meant,

No love that in a family dwells,
    No carolling in frosty air,
45   Nor all the steeple-shaking bells
    Can with this simple truth compare –
That God was Man in Palestine
And lives today in Bread and Wine.

(John Betjeman, 1906-1984)

Poetry technique: Rhyme

Rhyme is the use of words which have the same endings such as 'dwells' and 'bells' or 'clang' and 'hang'. It applies to sound not spelling. So 'air' rhymes with 'compare'.

It can also apply to more than one syllable as in 'flowers' and 'towers' or, in *Death of an Aircraft*, 'stations' and 'relations' and 'condition' and 'ammunition'.

Poets frequently rhyme their line endings, sometimes in lines which follow each other and sometimes with lines which are further apart. In verse one of *Christmas*, for example, Betjeman rhymes 'again' with 'rain', and 'sheen' with 'green' but, oddly, there is no rhyme to link the first with the third line.

Look carefully at the pattern of the rhyme scheme in verse one of *Christmas* and compare it with the rhyme scheme in the other verses. Then compare it with the pattern in *Circus Lion* and *Death of an Aircraft*. Try to work out what effect the rhyme has on the meaning of the poem.

Sometimes poets also use rhyme to link words which are not at the ends of lines. 'Light' and 'night' rhyme in the third line of verse 1 for instance. This is known as **internal rhyme.**

Poetry like *Telephone Conversation*, which doesn't have rhymed line endings, is called **blank verse**.

Exercise 4.2

Read the poem *Christmas* and then answer these questions. Quote from the poem in your answer.

1.   What pre-Christmas preparations are described in the poem?

2.   What is the meaning of (a) Advent (line 1), (b) Corporation (line 14), (c) tenements (line 15)?

3.   Which details in the poem tell you that this poem was written in and about the 1950s?

4.   What do you think the poet is trying to say? Sum up the poem's message in your own words.

5. Look carefully at the poem's rhyme pattern. What does this add to the poem?

6. Comment on the phrases (a) pigeon-haunted classic towers (line 22), (b) hideous tie so kindly meant (line 42).

Save the Nativity Play

This is an article which was published at Christmas in a newspaper. It isn't a news item; it is a column expressing the writer's own views.

1 When our younger son, Felix, was about 6, he played a shepherd in his infant school's nativity play. He sang a solo in a high-pitched treble. Yes, it was lump in the throat stuff to see him in his little brown dressing gown with the inevitable check tea towel tied Arab-style on his head.

5 A generation later how many children will learn this Christmas what Felix learned from that experience? Regrettably, school nativity plays are now an endangered species. But they are a crucial part of real education and there's a great deal more to them than giving proudly weepy Mums and Grans an afternoon out.

The story of the birth, life and death of Jesus Christ has underpinned European culture
10 for two thousand years. Whether or not the Christian nativity story is literally true for you, it carries timeless messages for everyone.

That is its great strength. Family values, the conflict between good and evil and the reality of birth and death affect every man, woman and child in the world.

So all children in British schools should be taught about the background and the
15 meaning of Christmas and the nativity play is a good, participative way of doing it.

A skilled teacher can and should involve every child in the class. Christianity – its mythology, customs, beliefs and ideas – has lain at the heart of British culture for more than seventeen centuries. No young Briton should, therefore, be left in ignorance of its implications, regardless of his race, colour or creed.

20 To argue that Christmas is irrelevant just because a school has, say, a high proportion of Sikh pupils, is a nasty bit of racism.

The British citizen who is deliberately deprived of knowledge about his country's history and background is seriously disadvantaged. Schools should be sharing knowledge, not withholding it.

25 What does Christmas mean? Whatever your religion, or however fiercely atheist you might be, we can surely agree that Christmas has a lot to say about the conflict between good and evil?

Goodness is represented in Mary's quiet acceptance of the situation and in Joseph's astonishing forbearance. Then there's the excitement of the shepherds who came just
30 down the hill into Bethlehem.

And don't forget the wise men who travelled so determinedly such a long way. The 'angelic-ness' of Gabriel is pure goodness too and all of this can be better understood by taking part in a nativity play.

Human evil is rife: wars, atrocities, murders, rapes, cruelty, abuse, neglect. You need not
35 look far. September 11th and the war against Iraq are very recent history.

Herod and his thugs are evil, sinister and threatening. They represent worldly evil in the nativity story. Fearing an attempted political takeover by a 'new king,' he ruthlessly orders his soldiers to slaughter all infant boys. Many children die.

Yet there is hope in the nativity story. It's a way of teaching children that good can, and
40 does, overpower the evil it confronts.

Because of his closely-bonded family and a message from Gabriel, the force of goodness which pulls against the evil of Herod, the infant Jesus escapes with his family.

And that's something else the nativity play is about – families. Mary, Joseph and the child are a unit pulling together under difficult circumstances. Families come in many
45 shapes and forms. The Christian nativity story reminds us to value those closest to us. Another message for our times, surely?

Birth is a new beginning. But everyone who is born also eventually dies. There are pre-echoes in the nativity story of the dreadful, violent death by crucifixion which awaits Jesus, thirty-three years later.

50 Properly handled, a nativity play has a message for children about the inevitability of death – not an easy subject, but one which certainly shouldn't be ignored.

Yet, some schools have abandoned the nativity play tradition for namby-pamby reasons of political correctness. They dare not 'upset' children of other faiths and some teachers think it compromises their atheism.

55   I contend that the nativity message about human life and the indomitability of the human spirit matter a lot more than any individual's doctrinal squeamishness. This is nothing to do with indoctrination. It's about imparting inter-faith universal truths.

The nativity play has a long and respected history. St Francis of Assisi is thought to have invented it in the 13th century as a teaching aid. Don't let's casually throw it away now.

(Susan Elkin, in the *Daily Mail*, December 16th 2003)

Exercise 4.3

Answer these questions, referring to the words in the passage in your answer:

1.   Give another word for (a) literally (line 10), (b) atheist (line 25), (c) forbearance (line 29), (d) indomitability (line 55).

2.   What is St Francis believed to have done in the 1200s?

3.   Sum up in your own words the writer's reasons for wanting schools to put on nativity plays.

4.   Why are some schools now not doing nativity plays, according to the writer?

5.   Why do you think the writer begins her article with an anecdote about her own son?

6.   Explain what the writer means when she says that Jesus's biography has 'underpinned European culture for two thousand years' (lines 9-10).

7.   Pick out and comment on three ways in which Susan Elkin's style is different from Thomas Hardy's.

Exercise 4.4

Your turn to write:

1.   Write a story or poem about any aspect of Christmas you wish.

2.   Write a nativity story – or play – set in your community today.

3.   Write a letter to the *Daily Mail* disagreeing with Susan Elkin's view of nativity plays.

4.   Imagine you are either the girl at the window or Farmer Shinar in Thomas Hardy's Mellstock. Write a letter to a friend describing the visit of the carollers. Invent as much detail as you like.

5.   Some people argue that Christmas now focuses so much on buying things like presents, decorations and elaborate food that it has lost its true meaning. Do you agree? Write your views.

6.   Describe the celebration of Christmas in your school or in a school you have attended in the past. Make your writing as lively as you can.

Spell check

Verbs which end in '-y', if the letter before the 'y' is a **consonant** (like the nouns we looked at in Chapter 3) change the 'y' to 'ies' when we use that part of the verb which requires an 's'. So:

I deny	he denies
We apply	she applies
You defy	he defies
I dry	it dries

Verbs which end in '-y' but which have a **vowel** before it simply add 's' as required. So:

I play	it plays
We buy	he buys
You portray	she portrays
I enjoy	he enjoys

Exercise 4.5

Write these sentences, adding the correctly-spelled form of the given verb:

1.   Peter (fry) eggs for breakfast but Jack (enjoy) mushrooms more.

2.   'We must make sure he (purify) the water,' said the desert explorer of an assistant.

3.   Our cat (stray) further than we'd like him to.

4.   The school (supply) pupils with stationery but each boy or girl (try) not to waste it.

5.   That machine (amplify) the sound.

6.   Laura (deny) that she (buy) sweets but Hatty (say) she has seen her do so.

Make sure that you can spell these ten words taken form the passages above:

perceived	unconsciously	obliquely	appreciative	existence
righteousness	experience	irrelevant	beginning	crucifixion

Exercise 4.6

These 20 words are used in the three passages above. Carefully learn their spellings and then practise writing them in sentences.

perceived	concentrated	unconsciously	proclaimed	spiritual
obliquely	appreciative	existence	righteousness	tortoise
provincial	tremendous	inexpensive	experience	participative
irrelevant	atrocities	beginning	crucifixion	abandoned

Vocabulary

The word 'mythology' comes from the Greek words *muthos*, 'fable', and *logos*, 'word' or 'speech'. It means 'the body of knowledge and stories associated with a particular culture'.

A word ending with '-logy' or '-ology' usually now means the study of that subject. So we get words like 'zoology' which means 'the scientific study of animals' and 'psychology', 'the scientific study of the human mind'.

Exercise 4.7

Match the following '-ology' words to their meanings. Work out the ones which are obvious to you first and then use a dictionary to sort out the rest.

theology	study of birds
chronology	study of the stars
archaeology	study of human beings
neurology	study of the weather
ornithology	study of the nature of God
musicology	study of animals
zoology	study of history to establish dates
anthropology	study of the human nervous system
astrology	study of ancient history though excavation
meteorology	study of music as an academic subject

Synonyms

Susan Elkin wrote 'I contend' where she could just as easily have used **synonyms** such as 'believe', 'argue', 'suggest' or 'aver'.

English has many synonyms (words which are similar in meaning) but remember that:

1. words change their meaning according to context, so that two words may mean something similar in one context but not in another. For example, 'beat' means the same as 'overcame' in the sentence 'I beat/overcame my fear' but you cannot say 'I counted her heart-overcame' or 'I'll overcome the eggs for the omelette'.

    For another example, 'book' is a synonym for 'reserve' if you say 'I must book/reserve a table in the restaurant' but you cannot say 'I want to change my library reserve' or 'She's the book for the netball team'.

    You can make up lots of examples of this for yourself.

2. it is very unusual for two words to mean exactly the same as each other. 'Contend' suggests that the writer or speaker is stating something that he or she expects to be controversial – or contentious (the adjective related to the verb 'contend').

Exercise 4.8

Provide as many synonyms as you can for the marked words as they are used in these sentences. Try to do this without using a thesaurus.

1. Maria and Rasheed **walked** home.

2. John Betjeman **captures** the atmosphere of Christmas.

3. Christmas can be a **jolly** season.

4. I read **quickly**.

5. Our teacher insists on **courtesy** in the classroom.

6. When we saw the mess it was hard not to **giggle**.

Grammar and punctuation

A **preposition** tells you where a noun or pronoun is in relation to something else in the sentence. Prepositions are words such as:

John Betjeman capturing the atmosphere of Christmas

| around | behind | above | near | into |
| through | opposite | from | across | towards |

My friend lives **within** York's city walls.

Cameron had a letter **from** his mother.

We arranged our Christmas cards **along** the shelves.

Some prepositions need especial care:

among: Something is shared **among several** people.
between: Something is shared **between two** people.

beside means 'at the side of'. So: 'Henry stood **beside** the river.'
besides means 'in addition to'. So: 'Several boys were in the team **besides** Oliver.'

in shows the position in one place. So: 'Father Christmas was stuck **in** the chimney.'
into shows movement from one place to another. So: 'The reindeer tumbled **into** the garden.'

past is a preposition and is always used with a verb: 'The sleigh went **past** our house.' ('passed' is not a preposition but the past tense of the verb 'to pass'. So: 'The sleigh passed our house.')

Exercise 4.9

Make up sentences of your own, using the following prepositions carefully:

Remember that some of these words can also be used as other parts of speech. Your job here is to use them as prepositions.

1.	beyond	6.	without
2.	beside	7.	under
3.	during	8.	past
4.	after	9.	by
5.	among	10.	into

There are eight parts of speech (sometimes called word classes): **noun**, **verb**, **adverb**, **adjective**, **pronoun**, **conjunction**, **preposition** . . . and **article**.

Of these, the **article** is by far the simplest. Only three words in English are articles:

> **the**   a   an

'The' is the **definite article** because '**the** pudding' or '**the** Christmas tree' means a **specific** one.

'A' is the **indefinite article** because '**a** pudding' or '**a** Christmas tree' refers to **any** one.

'An' is just another form of the indefinite article. It means exactly the same as 'a' but is used when the next word begins with a vowel as it is easier to say. So '**an** umbrella', '**an** elephant', '**an** enormous balloon,' '**an** opened present'.

Sometimes 'an' is used before a word beginning with 'h', although this is becoming increasingly rare. For example you may find '**an** historian' or '**an** hotel'.

In each case, the article is modifying the noun which follows it by stating its definite or indefinite status.

Exercise 4.10

See how many shorter words of four letters and more you can make out of the words:

> DEFINITE ARTICLE.

Punctuating direct speech

When you punctuate direct speech, enclose all the words spoken in inverted commas (also called **speech marks** or **quotation marks**). You usually also need a comma, full stop, question mark or exclamation mark at the end of the words spoken. Begin a new paragraph every time a new person speaks.

Look carefully at these examples:

> 'Now to Farmer Shinar's, and then replenish our insides, Father,' said the tranter.

> 'Very unseemly – very!' said old William, as they retired.

> 'Where's Dick?' said old Dewy

Exercise 4.11

Write out the following conversation with its correct punctuation:

Mr Pickwick is about to try ice skating

It looks nice warm exercise that doesn't it he enquired of Wardle. Ah it does indeed replied Wardle. Do you slide? I used to do so on the gutters when I was a boy replied Mr Pickwick. Try it now said Wardle. Oh do please Mr Pickwick cried all the ladies. I should be very happy to afford you some amusement replied Mr Pickwick but I haven't done such a thing these thirty years.

(From *Pickwick Papers* by Charles Dickens, 1836-37)

Speaking and listening

1. Get your class to find as many Christmas poems as you can. Learn and rehearse one each. Then organise a Christmas poetry festival in which you all speak and share your poems. You could invite another class to share this with you.

2. Organise a class discussion or debate about what Christmas means to you and what it should mean.

3. With adult permission and advice, interview an older person (one of your grandparents or great-grandparents, perhaps?) about how Christmas was celebrated when he or she was young. Alternatively, find someone to interview who has spent his or her childhood in another country.

4. With your teacher's agreement, invite to your classroom someone with strong views about Christmas, perhaps a vicar, or a nurse who works over Christmas, or a shopkeeper who relies on the higher takings that Christmas brings. Prepare questions to ask your guest. One of the class should introduce him or her and another should sum up and thank the guest at the end.

Have you read?

These books are all either about Christmas or include Christmas as part of the story:

Under the Greenwood Tree by Thomas Hardy (1872)
Puffin Book of Christmas Stories ed. Wendy Cooling (2001)
Oxford Book of Christmas Stories ed. Dennis Pepper (1986)
A Child's Christmas in Wales by Dylan Thomas (1955)
Oxford Book of Christmas Poems ed. Michael Harrison & Christopher Stuart-Clark (1983)
A Christmas Carol by Charles Dickens (1843)
Little Women by Louisa M Alcott (1869)
A Castaway Christmas by Margaret J Baker (1965)

Silent Snow, Secret Snow by Adele Geras (2003)
The Family from One End Street and Some Of Their Adventures by Eve Garnett (1937)
Goodnight Mr Tom by Michelle Magorian (1981)
The Wind in the Willows by Kenneth Grahame (1908)

And if you've done all that

● Thomas Hardy took the title *Under the Greenwood Tree* from a poem by William Blake. Another of his novels *Far From the Madding Crowd* takes its title from the poem *Elegy in a Country Churchyard* by Thomas Gray. Writers often 'borrow' their titles from other writers. Find out who wrote the following and where each title comes from: *Brave New World*, *Things Fall Apart*, *Murder Most Foul*, *Devices and Desires*, *Of Mice and Men*.

● How many more examples can you add to the list? Consider film and music titles too.

● In Betjeman's poem, 'Hooker's Green' and 'Crimson Lake' are not places, they are artists' colours. Other glamorous-sounding colours include Prussian blue, vermilion, yellow ochre, carmine red and ultramarine. Invent as many original names for colours as you can. Then you could make them into a colour poem. (You could also use the ones listed here.)

● John Betjeman was Poet Laureate. Find out what this means. Prepare a short talk for the rest of your class about the office of Poet Laureate and its history.

● Here is another Christmas poem just for fun. Discuss it with a friend and then perform the poem to the rest of the class.

Reindeer Report

Chimneys: colder.
Flightpaths: busier.
Driver: Christmas (F)
Still baffled by postcodes.

Children: more
And stay up later.
Presents: heavier.
Pay: frozen.
Mission in spite
Of all this
Accomplished.

(U.A. Fanthorpe, born 1929)

Chapter 5

Love

Silas Marner, then a lonely weaver, adopted Eppie when she was eighteen months old because her mother had collapsed and died in the snow near his cottage.

1   'Father,' said Eppie very gently, after they had been sitting in silence a little while. 'If I was to be married, ought I to be married with my mother's ring?'

   Silas gave an almost imperceptible start, though the question fell in with the under-current of thought in his own mind, and then, in a subdued tone, 'Why, Eppie, have you
5   been a-thinking on it?'

   'Only this last week, Father,' said Eppie ingenuously, 'since Aaron talked to me about it.'

   'And what did he say?' said Silas, still in the same subdued way as if he were anxious lest he should fall into the slightest tone that was not for Eppie's good.

   'He said he should like to be married, because he's a-going in four-and-twenty, and had
10   got a deal of gardening work, now Mr Mott's given up. And he goes twice a week regular to Mr Cass's, and once to Mr Osgood's, and they're going to take him on at the Rectory.'

   'And who is it as he's wanting to marry?' said Silas with rather a sad smile.

   'Why, me to be sure Daddy,' said Eppie, with dimpling laughter, kissing her father's cheek, 'as if he'd want to marry anybody else!'

15   'And you mean to have him, do you?' said Silas.

   'Yes, some time,' said Eppie, 'I don't know when. "Everybody's married some time," Aaron says. But I told him that wasn't true: For I said, "Look at Father. He's never been married."'

   'No child,' said Silas, 'your father was a lone man till you was sent to him.'

20   'But you'll never be lone again, Father,' said Eppie tenderly. 'That was what Aaron said – "I could never think o' taking you away from Master Marner, Eppie." And I said, "It 'ud be no good if you did, Aaron." And he wants us all to live together, so as you needn't work a bit, Father, only what's for your own pleasure. And he'd be as good as son to you – that was what he said.'

25   'And should you like that, Eppie?' said Silas, looking at her.

   'I shouldn't mind it, Father,' said Eppie, quite simply. 'And I should like things to be so as you needn't work much. But if it wasn't for that, I'd sooner things didn't change. I'm very happy: I like Aaron to be fond of me and come and see us often, and behave pretty to you – he always *does* behave pretty to you, doesn't he, Father?'

30   'Yes, child, nobody could behave better,' said Silas, emphatically. 'He's his mother's lad.'

'But I don't want any change,' said Eppie. 'I should like to go on a long, long while just as we are. Only Aaron does want a change; and he made me cry a bit – only a bit – because he said I didn't care for him. For if I cared for him I should want us to be married, as he did.'

35   'Eh my blessed child,' said Silas, laying down his pipe as if it were useless to pretend to smoke any longer, 'you're o'er young to be married. We'll ask Mrs Winthrop – we'll ask Aaron's mother what *she* thinks: if there's a right thing to do, she'll come at it. But there's this to be thought on, Eppie. Things *will* change, whether we like it or not. Things won't go on as they are for a long while just as they are and no difference. I

40   shall get old and more helpless and be a burden on you perhaps, if I don't go away from you altogether. Not as I mean you'd think me a burden – I know you wouldn't – but it 'ud be hard upon you: and when I look for'ard to that, I like to think as you'd have somebody else besides me – somebody young and strong, as'll outlast your own life and take care on you to the end.' Silas paused, and resting his wrists on his knees, lifted his

45   hands up and down meditatively as he looked on the ground.

'Then would you like me to be married, Father,' said Eppie, with a little trembling in her voice.

'I'll not be the man to say no, Eppie,' said Silas emphatically. 'But we'll ask your godmother. She'll wish the right thing by you and her son too.'

(From *Silas Marner* by George Eliot, 1861)

Exercise 5.1

Answer these questions as fully as you can.

1.   Explain the meaning of: (a) imperceptible (line 3), (b) subdued (line 4), (c) outlast (line 43).

2.   What is Aaron's family name?

3.   Summarise everything you learn from this passage about (a) Aaron and (b) his mother.

4.   Referring closely to the passage, explain in your own words what Silas feels about Eppie's proposed marriage.

5.   Why hasn't Eppie accepted Aaron's proposal?

6.   Write three sentences of your own using the adverbs (a) ingenuously, (b) emphatically and (c) meditatively to show that you understand their meaning.

Sonnet 18

Read this poem carefully several times both silently and aloud:

1   Shall I compare thee to a summer's day?
      Thou art more lovely and more temperate:
      Rough winds do shake the darling buds of May,
      And summer's lease hath all too short a date:
5   Sometimes too hot the eye of heaven shines,
      And often is his gold complexion dimm'd,
      And every fair from fair sometime declines,
      By chance, or nature's changing course untrimm'd;
      But thy eternal summer shall not fade,
10   Nor lose possession of that fair thou ow'st,
      Nor shall death brag thou wander'st in his shade,
      When in eternal lines to time thou grow'st;
         So long as men can breathe, or eyes can see,
         So long lives this, and this gives life to thee.

**(William Shakespeare 1564-1616;
Shakespeare's 154 sonnets were first published in 1609)**

Poetry technique: Metre

Poetry can be seen as notes and spaces which come together to make a 'tune' in exactly the same way as music does. In music, different time signatures give you different sorts of melody, such as a march, a waltz or a hornpipe.

In a similar way different arrangements of **metre,** as it is called in poetry, give you different sorts of poem.

Shakespeare's sonnet has five feet (the equivalent of bars in music) in each line:

    So long / as men / can breathe / or eyes / can see
    So long / lives this / and this / gives life / to thee

*Mr Shakespeare trying out
one of his lines with five feet*

A line of poetry with five feet is called a **pentameter**. (Compare the word **pent**ameter with **pent**agon, **pent**athlon, and the delightful word **Pent**ateuch – which means the first five books in the Bible.)

Say the last two lines of Shakespeare's sonnet aloud several times. Listen to where you are putting the stresses or accents:

> So **long** / as **men** / can **breathe** / or **eyes** / can **see**
> So **long** / lives **this** / and **this** / gives **life** / to **thee**

Two syllables in which the first is a light 'upbeat' and the second a heavier syllable emphasised by the speaker are together known as an **iamb**.

Say 'by chance' and 'but thy' aloud and listen to where your voice falls. Words like 'hello' 'mistake' and 'suppose' are iambs too.

Because Shakespeare uses iambs and pentameters, we say that this sonnet (just as many poems and plays in English, including the text of Shakespeare's plays) is written in **iambic pentameters**. That is its metre.

Iambic pentameters tend to flow very easily because they are close to the natural rhythms of spoken English:

> I left my brolly on the northern line.

> Are you and I to meet for tea today?

> Suppose we ask for help to do our prep?

These pretty ordinary sentences are perfect examples of iambic pentameters. Try making up some of your own.

Exercise 5.2

Now answer the following questions. Use short quotations from the poem in your answers.

1. To whom do you think the poet is speaking?

2. Summarise what he is saying to her.

3. What is (a) 'the eye of heaven' (line 5) and (b) 'thy eternal summer' (line 9)?

4   Explain the meaning of 'And summer's lease hath all too short a date' (line 4).

5. Look carefully at the rhyme pattern of this sonnet. Why do you think Shakespeare rhymes 'shines' with 'declines' (lines 5 and 7) and 'fade' with 'shade' (lines 9 and 11)?

6. What is the meaning of the last rhyming couplet (the last two lines)?

St Valentine

Read carefully this factual passage, taken from a reference book:

St Valentine is the patron saint of lovers. He died around 269 AD.

1   There are in fact two Valentines, whose feasts are both celebrated on February 14th in the Roman martyrology[1], neither of whom has any obvious connection with loving couples.

    The first was a Roman priest and doctor who is believed to have been martyred under
5   Claudius II on the Flaminian Way where a basilica was erected in his honour in 350 AD.

    The other was a bishop of Turni (about 60 miles from Rome) who was brought to Rome, then tortured and executed there in about 272 AD, at the command of Placidus, the ruling prefect.

    Some people believe that the two Valentines are in fact one person – that the Roman
10   priest became the Bishop of Turni who was condemned in Turni and then brought to Rome for his sentence to be carried out. It is all, however, conjecture, because there is no reliable evidence.

    The present popularity of Valentine's Day has little to do with the historical saint or saints. From at least the time of Geoffrey Chaucer, the 14th century author of *The*
15   *Canterbury Tales*, people believed that birds begin to choose their mates on Valentine's feast day at the very beginning of spring. This is probably the origin of the tradition of choosing one's object of love on February 14th as a 'Valentine'.

    No British church is thought ever to have been dedicated to St Valentine, but he is often represented in art with a disabled or epileptic child at his feet whom he is thought to
20   have cured. Other depictions show him being beheaded for refusing to worship idols, which is what led to his martyrdom.

    As well as being associated with lovers, Valentine is also the patron saint of bee-keepers, travellers, the young and sufferers from epilepsy, fainting and plague.

Notes:
[1] list of martyrs. A martyr is someone who dies for his or her beliefs.

(Adapted from *The Wordsworth Dictionary of Saints* by Alison Jones)

Exercise 5.3

Now answer these questions:

1.   Roughly how long had Valentine (either one) been dead when the memorial was erected in the Flaminian Way?

2. Give another word for (a) conjecture (line 11), (b) dedicated (line 18), (c) depictions (line 20) as they are used in this passage.

3. Who wrote *The Canterbury Tales* and when?

4. Where is Turni?

5. Explain in your own words the probable reason for the link between February 14th and lovers.

6. Why do you think no British church has been named after St Valentine?

Exercise 5.4

Your turn to write:

1. Write a description of the atmosphere in your school on Valentine's Day.

2. Write a story about people falling in love with other people, with things, places or with anything you wish.

3. Write a conversation between a mother and son about the girl he loves and their future. This could be Mrs Winthrop and Aaron from *Silas Marner*, if you wish.

4. Write in any way you like, taking either 'The Darling Buds of May' or 'Eternal Lines to Time' as your title.

5. Write the story of Valentine as colourfully as you can. Use your imagination to fill in the details.

6. Write a poem addressed to something or someone you love.

7. Write a story about, or a factual account of, someone in the present day suffering (or dying) for his or her beliefs.

Spell check

Adjectives which end in '-y' change the 'y'; to 'i' when they take the suffix '-ness', provided that the letter before the 'y' is preceded by a **consonant** (as it usually is). So:

pretty	prettiness
steady	steadiness
happy	happiness
weary	weariness

An adjective such as 'grey' which has a **vowel** before the y simply adds '-ness' to make 'greyness'.

Exercise 5.5

List as many '-y' adjectives as you can; then write the correctly spelled noun ending in '-ness' next to each.

Make sure that you can spell the following ten words taken from the passages above:

anxious	useless	laughter	possession	connection
executed	condemned	beginning	associated	martyr

Vocabulary

The word 'martyr' is a **noun**.

As so often in English, several other words (such as 'martyrology') have developed from it:

'To martyr' is a **transitive verb** (one which requires an object to complete it).

e.g.   Placidus made the decision **to martyr** Valentine.
       The English army **martyred** Joan of Arc.

'Martyrdom' is another noun meaning 'the state of being martyred'. Compare it with 'freedom' ('the state of being free') or 'wisdom' ('the state of being wise'). The suffix '-dom' has found its way into more modern words too, such as 'stardom' and 'officialdom'.

Another suffix often added to words in English to mean a group of people or condition or quality is '-hood'.

Exercise 5.6

Use the following '-hood' words in sentences of your own:

1.   falsehood
2.   livelihood
3.   brotherhood
4.   likelihood
5.   priesthood
6.   neighbourhood

'Outlast' is an example of a new word which was formed in the past from an **adverb** or **preposition** and a **verb**. It probably once had a hyphen. Today it is a single word. 'Outclass', 'outgrow', 'outdate', 'outbid' and 'outdo' are other examples. Sometimes such words then turn into **nouns** such as 'outcast' and 'outcome'. Language never stands still!

Exercise 5.7

List as many verbs as you can which begin with the prefixes 'over-' and 'under-'.

Grammar and punctuation

Aaron usually **turns up** (arrives) at Silas and Eppie's cottage on Sunday afternoons.

Mr Jarvis **stood down** (resigned) from the committee.

We all **look up to** (admire) Shakespeare.

May I **get down** (descend) from the table?

These are examples of **phrasal verbs**. A specific **verb** and a particular **preposition** have come together and acquired a new meaning. There is almost always an alternative single word (shown in brackets in the sentences above). Overall though, we use phrasal verbs a great deal in everyday English because the alternative often seems too stilted and formal, especially in conversation.

Many phrasal verbs have acquired new meanings in addition to their original ones:

She **turned down** the bedcovers before getting into bed.

Miss Lang **turned down** the job offer.

We always **stand up** when the headmaster comes in.

I had to **stand up** for my friend because he was in trouble.

Although first language English speakers learn phrasal verbs quite easily as they grow up, non-native speakers usually find them difficult.

Exercise 5.8

Consider the meaning of the following phrasal verbs:

sit down	sit up	sit back	sit out	sit at
ask out	ask around	ask in		
take in	take out	take up		

Now use them to write some sentences of your own.

Exercise 5.9

Supply a more formal or more direct word for the phrasal verbs used in these sentences:

1. I felt my father **pull back** when he saw the slow lorry in front.

2. Amy wants to **give up** French.

3. Jonathan decided to **put in** for the position of Head Boy.

4. The angry doctor **walked out** of the meeting.

5. We'll sing hymn number 214 but we will **leave out** the third verse.

6. The cricket captain had to ask one of the reserves to **stand in** at the last moment.

Exercise 5.10

Don't forget the basic rules which govern the **apostrophe**:

- to replace missing letters: wouldn't, isn't, o'clock, it's (meaning 'it is' or 'it has') S'hampton;

- to show singular possession: one boy's pen (remember that this originated as 'one boy his pen');

- to show plural possession: all the girls' hockey sticks, several lovers' rings.

Write out the following sentences, adding the correct apostrophes:

1. Theyve reached home earlier than wed expected.

2. Freds cat and Mauras dog seemed to be making friends.

3. Ive just finished reading George Eliots *Adam Bede* and shall now begin Wilkie Collinss *The Woman in White*.

4. My three school dresses are all too small so were going to put them away in my younger sisters wardrobe.

5. *Lovers Vows* is the name of an old play which features in Jane Austens *Mansfield Park*.

6. Boys names and girls names are listed in the back of my Grannys dictionary.

Note that, where a noun ends in 's', the 's' after the apostrophe is sometimes omitted. For example, one sees both 'Jesus's name' and 'Jesus' name'.

Speaking and listening

1. Work with a partner. One of you should be Silas and the other Eppie. Rehearse their conversation as it is written in the above extract. They should – Silas in particular – have rural Midlands accents, if you can manage them!

2. Learn by heart *Sonnet 18* – one of the most beautiful and famous poems in English. Recite it as warmly as you can for a group or for the rest of the class.

3. Organise a small group discussion about Valentine's Day. Is it just a way for greetings card manufacturers and gift shops to make money, or does it have real meaning? Share your group's views with the rest of the class.

4. Prepare an individual talk about a saint, other than Valentine. Use a dictionary of saints or the Internet. There are some remarkable ones to choose from. You might then be able to use this for a school assembly.

Have you read?

The following books – some of them very famous – all have some kind of love interest. Please don't assume that this makes them 'girls' books' because they most definitely are NOT!

Silas Marner by George Eliot (1861)
Gone With the Wind by Margaret Mitchell (1936)
Pride and Prejudice by Jane Austen (1813)
The Woman in Black by Susan Hill (1983)
A Town Like Alice by Nevil Shute (1950)
Tristan and Iseult by Rosemary Sutcliff (1971)
Wuthering Heights by Emily Brontë (1847)
Junk by Melvyn Burgess (1996)
Rebecca by Daphne du Maurier (1938)
Tiger Eyes by Judy Blume (1981)
Postcards From No Man's Land by Aidan Chambers (2001)
The Shell House by Linda Newbery (2002)

And if you've done all that

- Write a 'hate' sonnet beginning 'Shall I compare thee to a winter's night?'. Follow Shakespeare's rhyme scheme and line pattern as closely as you can.

- Use the Internet or reference books to find out about the following famous pairs of lovers: Darby and Joan, Dido and Aeneas, Bonnie and Clyde, Antony and Cleopatra, Dante and Beatrice, Victoria and Albert. Make a 'Famous Couples' display area in your classroom. There are many others you could add.

- One of the most famous pieces of 'love music' ever written is Richard Wagner's *Liebestod*, part of his opera *Tristan und Isolde* (written 1857-59). It 'describes' the tragic moment when the lovers are finally separated. Borrow it from a music library or ask the school music department for a copy. Listen to it carefully several times and work out for yourself how successful you think it is.

Chapter 6

Growing Up

On their way from Charleston in South Carolina in the USA to visit an uncle in Australia, Mary and Peter are plane-wrecked alone on the Sturt Plain in the Northern territory of Australia. It is a remote area the size of England and Wales combined and it is almost uninhabited.

1   The hours meandered past like slow, unhurrying snails. At last the boy's head dropped to his sister's lap. He snuggled closer. His breathing became slower, deeper. He slept.

But the girl didn't sleep: that would never have done; for she had to keep guard. She was the elder. The responsibility was hers. That was the way it had always been, as far
5   back as she could remember. Always she had been the big sister who sticks plasters on Peter's knees, had taught him to tie his shoe-laces, and had taken the lead in their games of Indians and cowboys. Now that they were lost – somewhere in the middle of an unknown continent – the weight of her responsibility was greater than ever. A wave of tenderness welled up inside her. Always she had big-sistered him; now she must mother
10   him as well.

For a while she sat staring into the darkness; the darkness was warm, thick and almost tangible. Soon her mind became utterly blank. The day's events had been too overwhelming; had drawn on her too heavily. The rhythmic beat of the small boy's slumber came to her lullingly now. Gradually her breathing fell in step with his. The
15   whisper of the creek came to her like the croon of a lullaby. Her eyelids drooped and closed, fluttered and closed again. Soon she was fast asleep.

                              *   *   *

In the darkness beyond the gully, the bush came slowly to life.

A lumbering wombat came creeping out of his ground den. His short stumpy body forced a way through the underscrub; his long food-foraging snout ploughing through
20   the sandy earth in search of his favourite roots. Suddenly he stopped: sniffed: his nostrils dilated. He followed the new strange scent. Soon he came to the gully. He looked the children over, thoughtfully not hungrily for he was a vegetarian, an eater of roots. His curiosity satisfied, he shambled slowly away.

Random fireflies zigzagged by: their nightlights flickering like sparklets from a roving
25   toy-sized forge.

Soon, creeping along the edge of the darkness came another creature: a marsupial tiger-cat, her eyes widened by the night to glowing oriflames of fire. She too had scented the

children; she too clambered into the gully and looked them over. They smelt young and tender and tempting: but they were large; too bulky, she decided to drag back to her
30 mewling litter. On velvet paws she slunk away.

A night mist tried to gather: failed – for the air in the gully was too warm – and dissipated into the pre-dawn dew. The dampness settled on the children, pressing down their clothes, tracing the outlines of their clothes in tiny globules of pearl. They stirred but didn't wake. They were lost in their dreams.

35 In her sleep the girl moved uneasily. She was in the aeroplane again, and she knew that something was wrong. She and Peter were the only passengers, sandwiched between the crates of vegetables and the frozen carcasses of beef, and she was watching the port engine, waiting for the flames she knew would come. Too soon they were there; the tiny tongues of red licking out of the cowling. In her sleep she twisted and moaned. Then
40 mercifully her mind went blank – nature's safety valve that protects even in dreams those who have been shocked beyond endurance – and the next thing she dreamt was that she and Peter were staggering away from the blazing plane, she pulling him frantically because one of his legs was numb and his feet kept sinking into the soft yielding sand. 'Quick, Peter,' she gasped. 'Quick, before it explodes.' She heard a dull
45 pulsating roar, and looking back saw the figure of the Navigating Officer carrying the pilot and clambering out of the wreckage. In the heat of the explosion he gleamed white-hot, disintegrating. Again her mind went numb, but in her sleep, she clutched her brother's hand, clutched it and squeezed it so tight that he half-woke and slid awkwardly off her lap.

50 The nightlights of the fireflies became pale and anaemic. Out of the east crept a permeating greyness; a pearly opaqueness in the sky; the sun-up of another day.

(from *Walkabout* by James Vance Marshall, 1959)

Exercise 6.1

Answer the following questions as fully as you can:

1. Explain the meaning of (a) meandered (line 1), (b) lullingly (line 14), (c) dissipated (line 32).

2. Find phrases in the passage which mean exactly the same as (a) large pupils gleaming orange, (b) low throbbing noise.

3. Why did (a) the wombat and (b) the tiger-cat show no further interest in the children?

4. Why does Mary feel responsible for Peter?

5. Sum up in a short paragraph the accident to the plane. Use your own words.

6. What is 'nature's safety valve'?

Life in a Liberty Bodice

In this extract from an autobiography, the author describes growing up in the 1920s

1   For most of 1924 I was 14, the awkward age when dreams of what one might be are
     light years away from what one is. Like many adolescents of that and this period, I was
     awkward and shy with those who were unfamiliar but impudent and pert with those I
     knew well. But not with parents and their friends; it was a heinous sin 'to answer back.'
5   Elders were always assumed – often inaccurately – to be our betters whom we had,
     without reasoning, to respect.

     My mother had brought us up to be clean and plain. Not in so many words, but she made
     it quite clear that beauty was elsewhere. She had no feminine penchant for dressing up,
     making up or making up to men although she looked engagingly feminine herself.
10   Beauty, as far as my mother was concerned, was quite distant from her daughters and I
     cannot remember any of us having one feature or talent praised. Beauty, in my mother's
     book, was something caught on the brush by a Burne-Jones, a Watts or a Rossetti and
     their limpid ladies were certainly not for man-handling.

     Unlike the Pre-Raphaelite ladies with their loose girdles and their close-fitting morals,
15   our English rose skins were too often blemished with a blackhead or a spot, a condition
     which evoked no sympathy from my mother who loftily assumed that it was a lack of
     washing. It was a lonely and nerve-wracking business, nose against the mirror, going
     into battle against any guilty pore and then trying to disguise it with an unhygienic dab
     from a secret powder compact.

20   So we grew up through those threshold years with a Kiplingesque idea that a
     schoolgirl's role and goal was to be a *man*, my son! How romance ever insinuated its
     way into our lives was to be marvelled at. But in a naïve way it did.

     My mother, as I have already told, had a genius for attracting into our home people who
     shared high-minded thoughts, words and music. Regular visitors were George
25   Wilkinson, a magnetic lecturer in English at the training College in Leeds, and our
     oldest cousin Austin, a superb raconteur of North and East Riding dialect, and, at that
     time, Second Master at Woodhouse Grove School.

     Throughout our childhood, our home vibrated with do-it-yourself entertainment, and we
     children – a captive audience – needed no persuading to change roles and become the
30   entertainers. Mr Wilkinson's repertoire of spoken verse excluded the obscure and the
     analytical for words flowed from him with joyous, compulsive rhythm as different from
     the elocution-of-the-day as a brook is from piped water. He had no academic snobbery
     but revelled in simple but shapely verse full of imagery, rhyme and rhythm. So, without
     reference to print, we absorbed and knew by heart the poems he constantly repeated at
35   our request. Of these I still remember Alfred Noyes' *Whither Away is the Spring Today?*,
     his *Go Down to Kew in Lilac Time,* George Meredith's *Love in a Valley,* and
     Swinburne's *When the Hounds of Spring are on Winter's Traces,* and how we frolicked

through de la Mare's *Three Jolly Farmers* and Lear's *Jumblies*. I am grateful that we had this free ride before being caught in the grip of modern intellectual poets whose
40   stark prosaic lines took much of the joy and the music out of verse-speaking.

We girls sparkled and responded to George Wilkinson – a charmer – but as he was married and middle-aged, he was reserved for relaxed hero-worshipping. The next best thing, as far as I was concerned, was his son, Peter, who though not as verbally romantic as his father, was accessible and approved of by my mother and cousin Austin.
45   Fortuitously for me he was also at Woodhouse Grove, a sixth form boarder, so it was easy to arrange a family visit of the Hydes and Mr Wilkinson to Woodhouse Grove with Austin as our host. My heart soared with the idea of Sunday tea and evening service at a boys' boarding school – *his* school.

(from *Life in a Liberty Bodice* by Christabel Burniston,
first published 1991. New edition 2004)

Exercise 6.2

Answer these questions as fully as you can:

1.   Find single words in the passage which mean (a) impolite (b) story teller (c) bare (d) passion.

2.   How old was Christabel Burniston when the new edition of her book was published?

3.   Explain what the author means by a 'free ride' (line 39).

4.   Summarise what the author liked about George Wilkinson.

5.   In which ways did the author and her mother disagree?

6.   What do you deduce from this passage about the women painted by Edward Burne Jones, George Frederick Watts and Dante Gabriel Rossetti?

Timothy Winters

Read this poem several times both silently and aloud:

1   Timothy Winters comes to school
      With eyes as wide as a football pool,
      Ears like bombs and teeth like splinters:
      A blitz of a boy is Timothy Winters.

5   His belly is white, his neck is dark,
      And his hair is an exclamation mark,
      His clothes are enough to scare a crow
      And through his britches the blue winds blow.

      When teacher talks he won't hear a word
10   And he shoots down dead the arithmetic-bird,
      He licks the patterns off his plate
      And he's not even heard of the Welfare State.

Timothy Winters has bloody feet
And he lives in a house on Suez Street,
15   He sleeps in a sack on the kitchen floor
And they say there aren't boys like him any more.

Old Man Winters likes his beer
And his missus ran off with a bombardier,
Grandma sits in the grate with a gin
20   And Timothy's dosed with aspirin.

The Welfare Worker lies awake
But the law's as tricky as a ten-foot snake,
So Timothy Winters drinks his cup
And slowly goes on growing up.

25   At Morning Prayers the Master helves
For children less fortunate than ourselves,
And the loudest response in the room is when
Timothy Winters roars 'Amen!'

So come one angel, come on ten:
30   Timothy Winters says 'Amen
Amen amen amen amen.'
Timothy Winters, Lord.

Amen

(Charles Causley (1917 – 2003) wrote this poem in the 1950s.)

Poetry technique: Symbolism

A **symbol** is an object which represents something much bigger and more important than itself. For example, although the Union Flag is literally just a piece of flapping, coloured fabric, it stands for Great Britain. It is a symbol of Britain. In the same way, a wedding ring is really only a small hoop of metal but it stands for, and is a symbol of, a marriage.

Poets and other writers often use symbolism to represent abstract ideas. In *Timothy Winters* the 'sack on the kitchen floor' is a symbol of his poverty. In *Sonnet 18* 'the darling buds of May' symbolise youthful beauty and in *Circus Lion* the bars represent the lions' loss of freedom.

Read through all the poems we have looked at so far in this book for other examples of symbolism.

Exercise 6.3

Answer these questions about Charles Causley's poem:

1. What aspects of Timothy's appearance suggest that there are problems at home?

2. Describe his family.

3. What is meant by 'the law's as tricky as a ten-foot snake' (line 22)?

4. Explain in your own words what you think Charles Causley means by the last verse.

5. What does the rhyme and rhythm in this poem add to your understanding of it?

6. (a) What does the poet mean by 'shoots down dead the arithmetic bird' (line 10)?
   (b) Why does he put it like this?

Exercise 6.4

Your turn to write:

1. Write a story which begins with a shipwreck or plane-wreck.

2. Write a news item for a newspaper about a plane crash.

3. Write about a family friend or other regular visitor to your home.

4. Write a poem about anything you like, modelled on *Timothy Winters* and with verse pattern and rhymes similar to those used by Charles Causley. You might start, for instance, 'Jessica Smithers comes to town with jeans as wide as a dressing gown . . .'

5. Write about growing up in any way you wish.

6. Is it harder to grow up in the 21st century than it was when your parents or grandparents were your age? Write your views.

Spell check

If 'all' is used as prefix, it has only one 'l'. So:

already   **al**though   **al**ways   **al**most   **al**together

Interestingly, each of these can also be used as two words, although the meaning and the grammar is different. For example:

Are we **all ready** for school? ('All' is an adverb and 'ready' is an adjective.)
Is it six o'clock **already**? ('Already' is an adverb.)

That is why it's particularly important to spell these correctly because – in this case – spelling affects meaning.

Exercise 6.5

Make up sentences using these pairs. Write one sentence for each (10 in total).

1. all though   although
2. all ways   always
3. all most   almost
4. all together   altogether

LEARN: 'all right' is TWO WORDS and **does not exist in any other form**.

Learn the spelling of the following ten words all taken from the passages above:

rhythmic	scented	disintegration	awkwardly	anaemic
adolescents	unhygienic	naïve	accessible	arithmetic

Exercise 6.6

Vocabulary

'Hygiene' comes from the name of the Greek goddess of health, *Hygeia*.

Many English words derive from Greek and Latin gods and goddesses, or from notable figures in mythology. Look up the following examples in a good dictionary and make a note of the meanings (if you don't know them) and origins of these words:

1. cereal   6. martial
2. mercurial   7. hypnotic
3. jovial   8. tantalise
4. venerate   9. Herculean
5. vulcanise   10. floral

A vegetarian (or herbivore), James Vance Marshall tells us, is an 'eater of roots'. He is, of course, describing an animal and we are probably more familiar with the word 'vegetarian' when it is applied to human beings.

Exercise 6.7

Write out the following sentences using the correct '-arian' words from the list to fill in the gaps:

egalitarian	grammarian	nonagenarian	librarian
antiquarian	disciplinarian		

1. I found a wonderful old copy of *Oliver Twist* in an _____ bookshop.

2. The class was relieved to find its new teacher much less of a _____ than its old one.

3. We lit 90 candles on our granny's birthday cake to celebrate her becoming a _____.

4.   Britain has a much more ____ system of electing its government than many developing countries.

5.   Anyone who studies English from this book is well on his or her way to becoming a ____ !

6.   The ____ is responsible for all the new book purchases in our school.

Exercise 6.8

Write sentences of your own to show you understand the meaning of:

1.   septuagenarian   4.   authoritarian
2.   fruitarian   5.   veterinarian
3.   sectarian   6.   agrarian

Grammar and punctuation

There are three sorts of sentence:

1.   These are **simple** sentences:

He slept.
She was the elder.

Each has one subject, one verb and makes single statement.

Do not misuse the word 'simple' when you apply it to sentences. In grammar this is its precise meaning.

2.   This is a **compound** sentence:

He had no academic snobbery but revelled in simple but shapely verse, full of imagery, rhyme and rhythm.

It makes two equally weighted statements: (i) 'He had no academic snobbery.' and (ii) 'He revelled in simple but shapely verse, full of imagery, rhyme and rhythm.'

The statements are hooked together with the conjunction 'but'.

A compound sentence is one in which two or more statements are joined with conjunctions.

Here is another example:

They stirred but didn't wake.

A conjunction joining two statements together

3.   This is a **complex** sentence:

> My mother, as I have already told, had a genius for inviting people into our home who shared high-minded thoughts, words and music.

The main statement is: 'My mother had a genius for inviting people into our home'.

'As I have already told' and 'who shared high-minded thought, words and music' give extra information. They are groups of words – known as clauses – which act like adverbs and adjectives. They are called **subordinate clauses** because they are secondary to the sentence's main statement.

'As I have already told' is an **adverbial clause** because it adds to the meaning of (or qualifies or modifies) the main verb 'had'.

'Who shared high-minded thoughts and words and music' is an **adjectival clause** because it adds to the meaning of (or qualifies or modifies) the word 'people'.

Exercise 6.9

Which of the types of sentence described above is each of the following?

1.   Charles, who loves cricket and football, has broken his leg.

2.   Maisie ran for help and Jamila looked after their sick friend.

3.   I adore chocolate, spaghetti, avocados and apple crumble.

4.   One twin is tall but the other is quite short.

5.   Our school, which was badly flooded during the holidays, cannot now open on time.

6.   She laughed.

7.   My sister, as you know, is very keen on disco dancing which she does on Tuesdays at a club in town.

8.   Paul cooked the meal but everyone helped him clear up.

Exercise 6.10

Build each of the following simple sentences into a compound one by adding other statements joined with conjunctions:

1.   I cried.
2.   My mother was furious.
3.   We were eating ice cream.
4.   Max is running.
5.   Let's ask Rina.

Exercise 6.11

Build each of the simple sentences in Exercise 6.10 into complex ones by adding adjectival and adverbial clauses.

Exercise 6.12

James Vance Marshall uses many colons (:) and semicolons (;).

As you may remember, a colon means 'as follows' or 'like this'; a semicolon is used in place of a full stop when the writer wants to stop but not fully. A semicolon is stronger than a comma but weaker than a full stop. When a semicolon is used, a full stop can almost always be substituted. It's a matter of taste and preference.

Working with a partner, read carefully through the extract from *Walkabout*. Look closely at every colon and semicolon.

Now edit it. Decide what changes you would make to the writer's punctuation.

Speaking and listening

1. Read one of the books in the *Have you read?* section. Spend two minutes trying to persuade the rest of the class to read it.

2. Interview an elderly person about his or her memories of growing up. (You could choose someone known to your family, to whom you talk out of school; alternatively, with your teacher's help, you could invite some interviewees into school.)

3. 'The hardest thing about growing up is . . .' Talk on this topic for one minute to a small group. Take it in turns.

4. With a partner discuss any aspect of growing up which interests you both.

Have you read?

All these books feature young people growing up:

Walkabout by James Vance Marshall (1957)
Life in a Liberty Bodice by Christabel Burniston (1991)
Collected Poems by Charles Causley (2000)
Sisterland by Linda Newbery (2003)
Catcher in the Rye by J D Salinger (1951)
A Gathering Light by Jennifer Donnelly (2003)
Great Expectations by Charles Dickens (1861)

The Diary of a Young Girl; Definitive Edition by Anne Frank (1947)
The Garbage King by Elizabeth Laird (2003)
Angela's Ashes by Frank McCourt (1999)
Cider With Rosie by Laurie Lee (1959)

And if you've done all that

- Read the rest of *Walkabout*. Then watch *Rabbit-Proof Fence*, a film now available on video and DVD. (It's probably in your public or school library.) What do you learn about the aboriginal people of Australia and their history from these two sources? Write an article for the school magazine and/or give a talk to the class on this topic.

- Find out everything you can about Burne Jones, G F Watts and Dante Gabriel Rossetti, the three artists mentioned by Christabel Burniston.

- Look at this anagram star:

Make as many words as you can with four letters or more by rearranging the letters in the star. Every word you make must include the letter in the centre. One of your words should use all 10 letters. Aim for 30 words.

Now invent anagram stars for your friends to work on. Use 7, 8, 9 or 10 letter words and work out the answers yourself before passing a puzzle on to anyone else.

Chapter 7

London

This passage comes from the first of the long and famous series of books about the amateur detective Sherlock Holmes. The narrator – Holmes's friend Dr Watson – describes a visit to a house in South London where a murder has taken place.

1   He hustled on his overcoat, and bustled about in a way that showed that an energetic fit had superseded the apathetic one.

'Get your hat,' he said.

'You wish me to come?'

5   'Yes, if you have nothing better to do.' A minute later we were both in a hansom[1], driving furiously for the Brixton Road.

It was a foggy, cloudy morning, and a dun-coloured veil hung over the house-tops, looking like the reflection of the mud-coloured streets beneath. My companion was in the best of spirits, and prattled away about Cremona fiddles, and the difference between

10   a Stradivarius and an Amati. As for myself, I was silent, for the dull weather and the melancholy business upon which we were engaged depressed my spirits.

'You don't seem to give much thought to the matter in hand,' I said at last, interrupting Holmes' musical disquisition.

'No data yet,' he answered. 'It is a capital mistake to theorise before you have all the

15   evidence. It biases the judgment.'

'You will have your data soon,' I remarked, pointing with my finger; 'this is the Brixton Road, and that is the house, if I am not very much mistaken.'

'So it is. Stop, driver, stop!' We were still a hundred yards or so from it, but he insisted upon our alighting, and we finished our journey upon foot.

20   Number 3, Lauriston Gardens wore an ill-omened and minatory look. It was one of four which stood back some little way from the street, two being occupied and two empty. The latter looked out with three tiers of vacant melancholy windows, which were blank and dreary, save that here and there a 'To Let' card had developed like a cataract upon the bleared panes. A small garden sprinkled over with a scattered eruption of sickly

25   plants separated each of these houses from the street, and was traversed by a narrow pathway, yellowish in colour, and consisting apparently of a mixture of clay and of gravel. The whole place was very sloppy from the rain which had fallen through the

night. The garden was bounded by a three-foot brick wall with a fringe of wood rails upon the top, and against this wall was leaning a stalwart police constable, surrounded
30 by a small knot of loafers, who craned their necks and strained their eyes in the vain hope of catching some glimpse of the proceedings within.

I had imagined that Sherlock Holmes would at once have hurried into the house and plunged into a study of the mystery. Nothing appeared to be further from his intention. With an air of nonchalance which, under the circumstances, seemed to me to border
35 upon affectation, he lounged up and down the pavement, and gazed vacantly at the ground, the sky, the opposite houses and the line of railings. Having finished his scrutiny, he proceeded slowly down the path, or rather down the fringe of grass which flanked the path, keeping his eyes riveted upon the ground. Twice he stopped, and once I saw him smile, and heard him utter an exclamation of satisfaction. There were many
40 marks of footsteps upon the wet clayey soil, but since the police had been coming and going over it, I was unable to see how my companion could hope to learn anything from it. Still, I had had such extraordinary evidence of the quickness of his perceptive faculties, that I had no doubt that he could see a great deal which was hidden from me.

(From *A Study in Scarlet* by Arthur Conan Doyle, 1887)

Notes:
[1] horse-drawn taxi-cab

Sherlock Holmes on the trail

Exercise 7.1

Answer these questions as fully as you can:

1. Explain the meaning of (a) superseded (line 2), (b) disquisition (line 13), (c) stalwart (line 29), (d) nonchalance (line 34).

2. Find single words in the passage which mean (a) close inspection, (b) an attitude of showing off, (c) crossed, (d) threatening.

3. What evidence is there in this passage that Holmes is a more intelligent man than Watson?

4.   Which seven adjectives in the first two sentences of the paragraph about number 3, Lauriston Gardens make it clear that nothing happy can have happened there?

5.   What does Holmes 'prattle' about on the journey (line 9) and why?

6.   What other people are present at Lauriston Gardens and what are they doing when Holmes and Watson arrive?

London: Its History

1   Londinium was founded by the Romans at a convenient crossing of the Thames, though it had been convenient for the local inhabitants too. Tacitus, a Roman historian, describes a flourishing trading city existing in AD 67. The area was marshy but there was a low hill, roughly where the Bank of England now stands, and it was here that the

5   Romans chose to build a typical Roman city, primarily for military reasons. Their forum was where Leadenhall market now stands.

The Romans believed that Britain was a kind of El Dorado, and that they'd make their fortune here. The river was navigable a long way inland, and tidal, which made it easy to get boats in and out.

10   England, at that time, was inhabited by a hodge-podge of tribes and small kingdoms, and the Romans had little difficulty subduing them – despite some noble efforts at defence. The locals assimilated Roman culture and, after a couple of hundred years, were more Roman than the Romans. When the Romans pulled out, pressured by frontier wars, the Saxons took over.

15   They hated living in the old walled Roman city and established their own city of long huts, roughly where Covent Garden is today. This duality still persists – the 'City' is essentially Roman Londinium, and 'Westminster' is the Saxon add-on.

When new invaders swept the country the Saxons and their kin moved back into the safety of the old Roman City, by then quite deserted, and it was here that London

20   originated.

By the time the Normans took over from the Saxons after 1066, the basis of the mercantile capital was already laid. A charter of citizens' rights and a confederation of tradesmen provided a counterweight to the aristocracy.

London was a leading trading port of western Europe. Merchants from Italy, the

25   Netherlands, France and Germany lived around the river, which had only one crossing – the Old London Bridge – until 1769. Food and wine came in. Wool and leather went out. Due to the wool trade's centre in East Anglia – near the old Boston – London was for a time England's second city. However, the establishment of merchants' guilds, with the mayor at their head, re-established London's place as capital.

30   These medieval guilds and livery companies still exist today and preserve fine buildings across the City. The Weavers' Company dates back to 1130, the Saddlers' Company

goes back to 1272, the Wax Chandlers' Company to 1358, though the Launderers' Guild was formed as late as 1960. Napoleon's jibe that Britain was 'a nation of shopkeepers' is true. And, with a living to defend from invaders, and trading routes and privileges to
35   protect overseas, it was unsurprising that they made doughty fighters – as the French learned to their cost at Crécy and Agincourt.

In Tudor times – after years wasted in wars of succession (which explains Henry VIII's desperate and bloody attempts to secure a male heir) – the Dissolution of the Monasteries and terrible religious persecutions led to poverty and mass unemployment.
40   And the Black Death and other plagues decimated the population.

However, by the late 16th century, the seeds of England's future as a world trading power were sown with the formation of the Trading Companies – The East India Company, The Muscovy Company, The Levant Company and the Turkey Company. These, which, along with Britain's naval prowess, saw management techniques still
45   venerated by world corporations, conquered the world. England was also at the forefront of the arts with a lively theatre and music scene.

The plague in 1665 and the fire in 1666 shook London out of its complacency, but also led to a wave of property development – which is still going on. Wren, Hawksmoor and other forerunners of Sir Richard Rogers were soon dominating the city skylines.

50   The redevelopment continued into the 18th Century with buildings like The Bank of England and most of the bridges across the Thames springing up. Tower Bridge was opened in 1894. The Victorians supervised the transformation of London into a modern city with sewers and an underground railway (1863). Overground railways (1836) and omnibuses (1855) crossed the city, and the port of London enjoyed a final flowering.

55   Despite the presence of the royal palaces, Westminster Abbey (a place of pilgrimage) and the country's first printing presses, Westminster really only came into its own in the 19th century and was granted the title of a City, with its own mayor, in 1900. Until the 1850s it was the haunt of criminals, who used the sanctuary laws to hide in the precincts of Westminster Abbey. The redesigning of the area under Charles Barry put paid to this
60   unsavoury aspect and saw an expansion which coincided with the arrival of the railways. Nearby Victoria Station occupies the site of several private railway stations which were amalgamated in 1899.

The two World Wars saw huge destruction, both to the people and to the city, and some unfortunate rebuilding followed, with little real conservation work. Many of the city's
65   worst buildings date from this time, when the Greater London Council changed the face of the old city forever. It is said that the GLC did more damage to London than the Luftwaffe[1].

(Abridged from www.londontourist.org**)**

Notes:
[1] German airforce

Exercise 7.2

Answer these questions as fully as you can:

1. Which nineteenth century architect redesigned the Westminster area?

2. What did the Romans find practical about Londinium?

3. In what sense, according to this author, are the British a 'nation of shopkeepers' (line 33)?

4. What happened at Crécy and Agincourt?

5. What were England's major exports in medieval times?

6. Explain in your own words what the author means by 'The GLC did more damage to London than the Luftwaffe' (lines 66-67).

7. How did the sense that London is two cities – Westminster and the City of London – begin?

8. Summarise the difficulties experienced by Londoners in Tudor times.

Composed upon Westminster Bridge

September 3 1802

1   Earth has not anything to show more fair:
       Dull would he be of soul who could pass by
       A sight so touching in its majesty:
       This city now doth, like a garment, wear
5   The beauty of the morning, silent, bare,
       Ships, towers, domes, theatres and temples lie
       Open unto the fields, and to the sky;
       All bright and glittering in the smokeless air.
       Never did sun more beautifully steep[1]
10   In his first splendour, valley, rock or hill;
       Ne'r saw I, never felt, a calm so deep!
       The river glideth at his own sweet will:
       Dear God! the very houses seem asleep;
       And all that mighty heart is lying still.

(William Wordsworth, 1770-1850)

Notes:
[1] soak

Poetry technique: Personification

Personification is a specific sort of metaphor in which a comparison is made between something inanimate and a human being. When something is being compared with a person, it is **personified.**

In 'This city now doth like a garment wear . . .' Wordsworth is personifying the city by imagining it as a human being who can 'wear the beauty of the morning'.

Later in the poem he personifies first the river and then the houses too. Work out where this happens.

Compare these examples of personification with John Betjeman's treatment of London in the fourth verse of *Christmas* and with Wole Soyinka's presentation of Voice in the seventh line of *Telephone Conversation*.

(What is the metre of *Composed on Westminster Bridge*? Look at it carefully and compare it with Shakespeare's Sonnet 18.)

A metaphor comparing a city to a lady

Exercise 7.3

Answer these questions. Use your own words and quotations from the poem.

1. What time of day is it in Wordsworth's sonnet and how do you know?

2. Pick out four individual words which suggest that Wordsworth is enthusiastic about what he is seeing.

3. Wordsworth uses personification four times in this poem. Find these four times and say for each whether you think the description is effective and why.

4. What buildings can Wordsworth see?

5. Which phrase in the poem tells you that London was much smaller in 1802 than it is now?

Exercise 7.4

Your turn to write:

1. Describe a visit to London based on your own experience.

2. Write about a place in London and someone's arrival there. Make the details as sinister as you can, so that the reader knows something unpleasant is about to happen.

3. Write a poem – perhaps a sonnet shaped like Wordsworth's *Composed upon Westminster Bridge* – about a place you know and like. It could be in London or it could be anywhere you wish.

4. Write about London or another city in any way you wish.

5. Write a leaflet advertising an attraction in London, or some other city which you know well. You can almost certainly get extra information from the Internet to help you with this.

6. Write a short story in which London plays an important part.

Spell check

MOST nouns ending in '–o' in the singular take 's' in the plural. That includes:

Words of Spanish and Italian origin and musical nouns:

poncho	ponchos
banjo	banjos
concerto	concertos
patio	patios

Abbreviated nouns:

photo	photos
disco	discos

Nouns which end in a double vowel in the singular:

studio	studios
zoo	zoos

HOWEVER, there are thirteen quite common words ending in '–o' which take 'es' in the plural. These are:

buffalo	buffaloes
cargo	cargoes
domino	dominoes
echo	echoes
hero	heroes
memento	mementoes
mosquito	mosquitoes
negro	negroes
potato	potatoes
tomato	tomatoes
tornado	tornadoes
torpedo	torpedoes
volcano	volcanoes

Exercise 7.5

These words all take '–s' when they become plural. Work out which of the three categories above they fit into.

lasso	soprano	kangaroo	tattoo	scenario
hippo	embryo	biro	radio	albino

N.B. Take care with these two words: **libretto**, plural: **libretti** and **virtuoso**, plural: **virtuosi**.

Learn the spelling of these ten words which are all used in the three passages above:

superseded	interrupting	developed	separated	extraordinary
assimilated	essentially	privileges	succession	techniques

Vocabulary

The word 'navigable' means 'able to be negotiated' by ship or boat. It comes from the Latin word *navis*, meaning 'ship'. From it we also get 'navy', 'navigate', 'navigator', 'navigation', 'navvy' and the splendid word 'navicular' which means 'boat-shaped'.

An 'eruption' is an 'outbreak' from the Latin words *e*, meaning 'out', and *ruptura*, 'a breaking'. We get 'rupture' from the same root, along with 'interrupt' (to 'break into' something) and 'abrupt' (suddenly 'breaking away').

Exercise 7.6

Choose six of the above *navis and ruptura* words and use them in sentences of your own to make the meaning clear.

Exercise 7.7

'Hodge-podge' means an 'assortment' or a 'jumble'. Like 'hotch-potch', it has found its way into the language because people like pairs of words which rhyme and/or alliterate (begin with the same sounds).

Use a good dictionary to find out the meanings and origins of these expressions:

1. namby pamby
2. hanky panky
3. wishy washy
4. willy nilly
5. shilly shally
6. niminy piminy
7. airy fairy
8. hocus pocus

Grammar and punctuation

Voice

All verbs are expressed in either the **active voice** or the **passive voice**. Voice is quite different from tense. Whatever tense you're using, you have to use one voice or the other.

Londinium **was founded** by the Romans.	(passive)
The Romans **founded** Londinium.	(active)
It **is said** that . . .	(passive)
People (or 'they') **say** that . . .	(active)
This book **has been read** by eleven pupils.	(passive)
Eleven pupils **have read** this book.	(active)
It **will be agreed** that term will end on 20th July.	(passive)
We **shall agree** to end term on 20th July.	(active)

It is a matter of reversing the subject and object. Clearly, the writer of the first example wanted – for emphasis – to start his piece with the word 'Londinium'.

There is scope for both voices in writing but note that:

1. The passive voice often needs the word 'by'. It usually uses more words and requires a more complex form of the verb.

2. The active form is usually more straightforward and direct and therefore generally better.

Politicians often hide behind the passive voice with expressions like 'It has been decided that . . .' rather than 'We have decided . . .' or 'I am asked by voters . . .' rather than 'Voters asked me . . .' The passive voice can be very evasive!

Exercise 7.8

Change the active voice to the passive in these sentences:

1. Before the end of the month, the architect completed the plans.

2. The hockey player hit the ball a long way with her stick.

3. Nathan made some biscuits.

4. In 1066, William of Normandy took London.

5. The motorcyclist knocked down the old lady.

6. Mrs Johnson cleared the electronic whiteboard.

Exercise 7.9

This passage is written in the passive voice. Notice how stilted and awkward it sounds. Change it to the active. You will have to change some words.

> The conservatory was erected by Mary Swavesey and her sisters. The site had been measured and levelled by Gail. The sections of the conservatory had been prepared by Emma. Then the conservatory was put in place by the three sisters working together. It had been ordered and paid for by Mr Newington. The sisters were praised by him for a fine piece of work.

Transitive and intransitive

All verbs are **transitive** or **intransitive**.

A transitive verb requires an object to complete its meaning.

An intransitive verb makes sense without an object.

For example:

> Tacitus **describes** . . . This needs 'a flourishing trading city' to complete its meaning.

> Number 3, Lauriston Gardens **wore** . . . This needs 'an ill-omened and minatory look' to complete its meaning.

'Describe' and 'wore' are transitive verbs.

Examples of intransitive verbs:

> The river **glideth**.

> Several private railway stations **were amalgamated**.

These are complete statements. No object is required.

Exercise 7.10

Add objects (be inventive!) to these sentences to complete their transitive verbs:

1.   The Victorians supervised . . .

2.   Omnibuses crossed . . .

3.   The Port of London enjoyed . . .

4.   I asked . . .

5.   We represented . . .

6.   My mother saw . . .

Look very carefully at the punctuation in the first half of the extract from *A Study in Scarlet* at the beginning of this chapter. It is a fine example of how to set out and punctuate direct speech.

Exercise 7.11

Write a short conversation between two people who are either travelling through London or discussing doing so. Take great care to punctuate it accurately.

Speaking and listening

1.   Collect as many poems as you can which have something to do with London. Organise a class festival of London poetry in which you all read out and share the poems you have found.

2.   Organise discussions in small groups on the topic: 'Which is best: town or country?' Make notes on your group's thoughts and prepare a notice board display with other groups in the class.

3.   Take it in turns to speak for one minute each on the best thing you've ever seen or done in London. When they do this on Radio 4's quiz programme *Just a Minute,* panellists have to speak without hesitation, repetition or deviation. Try it!

Have you read?

London plays a major part in all these books:

The Sign of Four (and other Sherlock Holmes stories) by A Conan Doyle (1897)
Little Soldier by Bernard Ashley (2001)
The Moonstone by Wilkie Collins (1868)
Coram Boy by Jamila Gavin (2000)
Oliver Twist by Charles Dickens (1838)
The Keys to the Street by Ruth Rendell (1996)
Girls Out Late by Jacqueline Wilson (1999)
Firedrake's Eye by Patricia Finney (1992)
Brick Lane by Monica Ali (2003)

And if you've done all that

●   Listen to *A London Symphony* by Ralph Vaughan Williams (1913) and/or Edward Elgar's *Cockaigne Overture: In London Town* (1901). The music department in your school may be able to help. Or refer to www.bbc.co.uk/radio3 Both pieces try to present the everyday sounds of London. Decide how well you think they work.

●   Read the famous descriptions of 17th century London – especially the Great Fire in 1666 – in the diaries of Samuel Pepys and John Evelyn. These should be in your school or public library.

●   Over the page is another poem about London first published in 1955. Read it several times and think about what it means and what's interesting about it. Then introduce the poem to the rest of the class.

Sunken Evening

The green light floods the city square,
  A sea of fowl and feathered fish,
  Where squalls of rainbirds dive and splash
And gusty sparrows chop the air.

Submerged, the prawn-blue pigeons feed
  In sandy grottoes round the Mall,
  And crusted lobster-buses crawl
Among the fountains' silver weed.

There, like a wreck, with mast and bell,
  The torn church settles by the bow,
  While phosphorescent starlings stow
Their mussel shells along the hull.

The oyster-poet, drowned but dry,
  Rolls a black pearl between his bones;
  The typist, trapped by telephones,
Gazes in bubbles at the sky.

Till, with the dark, the swallows run,
  And homeward surges tide and fret –
  The slow night trawls its heavy net
And hauls the clerk to Surbiton.

(Laurie Lee, 1914-1977)

Chapter 8

Drought

Jinda lives in a rural village in Thailand in the 1970s. A long drought has led to failure of the rice crop upon which the villagers depend.

1   Heat the colour of fire, sky as heavy as mud, and under both the soil – hard, dry, unyielding.

It was a silent harvest. Across the valley, yellow rice fields stretched, stooped and dry. The sun glazed the afternoon with a heat so fierce that the distant mountains shimmered

5   in it. The dust in the sky, the cracked earth, and the shrivelled leaves fluttering on brittle branches – everything was scorched.

Fanning out in a jagged line across the fields were the harvesters, their sickles flashing in the sun. Nobody spoke. Nobody laughed. Nobody sang. The only noise was wave after wave of sullen hisses as the rice stalks were slashed and flung to the ground.

10   A single lark flew by, casting a swift shadow on the stubbled fields. From under the brim of her hat Jinda saw it wing its way west. It flew to a tamarind tree at the foot of the mountain, circled it three times and flew away.

A good sign, Jinda thought. Maybe the harvest won't be so poor after all. She straightened up, feeling prickles of pain shoot up her spine, and gazed at the brown fields

15   before her. In all her seventeen years, Jinda had never seen a crop as bad as this one. The heads of grain were so light the rice stalks were hardly bent under their weight. Jinda peeled the husk of one grain open: the rice grain inside was no thicker than a fingernail.

Sighing, she bent to work. A trickle of sweat ran down between her breasts and into the well of her navel. Her shirt was stuck to her in clammy patches, and the sickle handle

20   was damp in her palm. She reached for a sheaf of rice stalks and slashed through it.

Reach and slash, reach and slash. It was a rhythm she must have been born knowing, she thought, so deeply ingrained was it in her.

Out of the corner of her eye, she saw the hem of her sister Dao's sarong, faded grey where once the bright flowered pattern had been. Dao was stooped even lower than the

25   other harvesters in their row and was panting slightly as she strained to keep up.

From the edge of the field came the sudden sound of a thin, shrill wail.

'Your baby's crying, Dao,' Jinda said.

Her sister ignored her.

'Oi's crying,' Jinda repeated. 'Can't you hear him?'

30 'I hear him.'

'Maybe he's hungry.'

'He's always hungry.'

'Why don't you feed him then?'

'Why don't you mind your own business?' Dao snapped.

35 'But couldn't you try?' Jinda insisted, as the wailing got louder. 'I think at least you should try.'

Dao slashed through a sheaf of stalks and flung them to the ground. 'When I want your advice, sister,' she said, 'I'll ask for it.'

They did not speak again for the rest of the afternoon. The baby cried intermittently, but
40 Jinda did her best to ignore it.

How different this is from past harvests, Jinda thought. Just three years ago before the drought, she and Dao had gaily chatted away as they cut stalks heavy with grain. They talked about what they might buy after the harvest – new sarongs, some ducklings, and a bottle of honey. And as they talked, the dark handsome Ghan had sung love songs
45 across the fields to Dao, until her face turned so red she had to run down to the river and splash cold water on it.

When Dao and Ghan were married the whole village attended the wedding. All that morning the hundred or so families of Maekung each took their turn to tie the sacred thread around the bridal couple's wrists, and after the elaborate wedding feast countless
50 couples, young and old, had danced the Ramwong until the moon rose high above the palm trees and the kerosene lamps were lit.

There had been so much of everything then, Jinda thought wistfully, so much food and rice wine, so much music and movement, and, best of all, so much laughter.

And now, just two very poor harvests later, there was never any laughter, nothing but
55 the whisper of sickles against dry stalks in parched fields. Ghan had left to work in the city even before their son was born, and Dao – poor Dao, Jinda thought, stealing a glance at her sister's grim face – Dao had become just a shadow of her former self.

(Slightly abridged from *Rice without Rain* by Minfong Ho, 1986)

Exercise 8.1

Now answer these questions as fully as you can:

1. Roughly how many people lived in the village of Maekung?

2. Why do you think Dao is reluctant to feed the baby?

3. What does Jinda miss most from earlier years?

4. Why did Ghan go to the city?

5. Write a paragraph of your own to describe the traditional Thai rice-harvesting scene in as much detail as you can.

6. What do the villagers do with the surplus rice crop in a good year?

7. Why do you think Minfong Ho describes Dao's wedding?

The Ancient Mariner

An old sailor, The Ancient Mariner, is describing his troubled travels at sea in Coleridge's long, famous poem, first published in 1798. The mariner believes – and so do the other sailors – that he has brought a terrible curse on the ship by shooting an albatross, a large white seabird.

1   The sun now rose upon the right:
    Out of the sea came he,
    Still hid in mist, and on the left
    Went down into the sea.

5   And the good south wind still blew behind,
    But no sweet bird did follow,
    Nor any day for food or play
    Come to the mariners' hollo!

    And I had done a hellish thing,
10   And it would work 'em woe:
    For all averred I had killed the bird
    That made the breeze to blow.
    Ah wretch! Said they, the bird to slay,
    That made the breeze to blow.

15   Nor dim nor red, like God's own head,
    The glorious sun uprist:
    Then all averred I had killed the bird
    That brought the fog and mist.
    'Twas right. Said they, such birds to slay,
20   That bring the fog and mist.

    The fair breeze blew, the white foam flew.
    The furrows followed free:
    We were the first that ever burst
    Into that silent sea.

25 Down dropt the breeze, the sails dropt down,
    'Twas sad as sad could be;
    And we did speak only to break
    The silence of the sea!

    All in a hot and copper sky,
30 The bloody sun, at noon,
    Right above the mast did stand,
    No bigger than the moon.

    Day after day, day after day,
    We stuck, nor breath nor motion;
35 As idle as a painted ship
    Upon a painted ocean.

    Water, water everywhere,
    And all the boards did shrink;
    Water, water everywhere,
40 Nor any drop to drink.

    And every tongue, through utter drought,
    Was withered at the root:
    We could not speak, no more than if
    We had been choked with soot.

**(Extract, slightly abridged, from *The Rime of the Ancient Mariner*
by Samuel Taylor Coleridge, 1772-1834)**

Poetry technique: Alliteration

The repetition of consonants or vowels at the beginning of words is known as **alliteration**. In the extract from *The Ancient Mariner*, 'furrows followed free' (line 22) and 'would work 'em woe' (line 10) are good examples of this.

If you look back at the other poems printed in this book, you will find plenty of examples of alliteration because it's one of the commonest devices poets use.

More important, however, than spotting examples is to identify the purpose and effect of alliteration whenever it is used. Ask yourself:

1. What does it add to the music of the poem?

2. What does it add to the meaning?

3. Would it be a worse poem without alliteration?

Apply these questions to any example you are studying.

N.B. Notice the wonderful effects Coleridge achieves with **internal rhyme** in *The Ancient Mariner*.

Exercise 8.2

Read the extract from *The Rime of the Ancient Mariner* very carefully several times. Now answer these questions:

1.   Is the ship heading north or south? How do you know?

2.   Why can the ship not proceed?

3.   The words (a) hollo (line 8) and (b) uprist (line 16) are **archaisms** (words no longer in everyday use). Work out their meanings from the poem and explain each of them in your own words.

4.   Coleridge's poem is written mainly in four-line verses. Why do you think he uses two six-line verses at this point?

5.   Pick two examples of alliteration and explain how each adds to the meaning of the poem.

6.   What do you think the rhyme adds to the poem?

India bitten by drought, but lack of rain is not the only cause

1   For the last 12 months, the villagers of Kundal, Rajasthan, North West India, have had nothing to eat but broth of maize soaked in water, called rabri. Many of their cattle have died. Driving through this southern part of the state, you occasionally pass a cow's skull by the side of the road.

5   'We have one month's supply of water left,' says one villager. 'After that? Maybe we'll die too.'

In this area, just three hours' drive from the tourist destination of Udaipur, there has been no monsoon rain for four years. One of the city's lakes – Udaipur is famous for its Lake Palace Hotel, which usually seems to float on the water's shimmering surface – is

10   dry, for the first time in living memory.

In these villages – home to tribal people, or *adivasis* – the fields are brown, with stumps of dead shoots just puncturing the surface. One hand pump serves up to 30 families, who live widely spread, in the surrounding area.

15
Now there is still some water. But overuse means the pressure is dropping rapidly.

The water table in this part of the state is now so low that, ironically, even rain can only be of limited help. The skies turn purply-black in the late afternoon and, even when a few fat splodges of water drop from the sky, the drought's firm bite continues to hold.

20   Even more ironic is that the lack of rain is only part of the reason why some have already died of starvation in other villages in Rajasthan. The economic policies which were brought in by the government of India in a bid for riches are keeping millions so impoverished and marginalised that, in a country with a grain surplus, lack of rain has become deadly.

'Drought should not be having this kind of impact. Mechanisation means there is less daily wage labour work available in the area, and so people simply do not have the
25   money to buy food in,' says Ginny Shrivastava, of Astha, a Christian Aid partner working in the area.

The government of Rajasthan has put some measures in place to help its people. Those who have been identified as most vulnerable are given drought rations. It has also established a 'drought relief work' programme, similar to the concept of 'food for work'.
30   However, just one person in a family of 10-12 is currently earning food under this scheme.

Shrivastava says: 'It's about educating people. People have rights – they just don't know it. They need to know that they are entitled to grain; that a government inspector has to come along to assess whether they really are in a desperate situation.'

Before Astha's involvement, the illiterate and geographically remote people of Kundal
35   did not know their rights. Now, 25 people in this village of 400 families are receiving emergency grain supplies: 5 kilos of maize and 5 of wheat, to last a week. One family in 10 is also benefiting from the drought relief scheme – in this case, dam construction.

This is certainly not an end to the villagers' problems – the ration shops are often closed, and what is given out is usually little more than chaff, as the best quality grains
40   are creamed off by the shop manager. But Kundal has now found a way to break open the safety nets which are supposed to protect it.

'We have realised our collective strength,' says one woman. 'Now we know that, although there is no water, we do have an opportunity to survive.'

(From the Christian Aid website, 2002; www.christian-aid.org.uk**)**

Exercise 8.3

Answer the following questions:

1.   Where is Kundal?

2.   In which year did Kundal last experience heavy rainfall?

3.   How much grain is each individual receiving per week as an emergency ration?

4.   Which government policy has made things harder for the villagers?

5.   What steps has the government taken to help the villagers?

6.   Explain in your own words the meaning of (a) illiterate (line 34) and (b) geographically remote (line 34).

Exercise 8.4

Your turn to write:

1. Describe any journey you have made on water.

2. Write a story about a community struggling with drought.

3. Imagine you are a local government official in Rajasthan. You have read the article on the Christian Aid website. Write a letter to a local newspaper defending your position.

4. Write a poem about how you would feel if affected by a situation such as the one described on pages 91-92.

5. Continue Jinda's story.

6. Write about drought in any way you wish.

Spell check

Adjectives which end in '-al' add 'ly' when they become adverbs, creating a double 'l'. So:

ironic**al**	ironic**ally**
geographic**al**	geographic**ally**
usu**al**	usu**ally**
practic**al**	practic**ally**

Verbs like 'aver' (meaning 'to state strongly') usually double their final 'r' when they take an '-ed' or an '-ing' suffix. So:

aver	ave**rr**ed	ave**rr**ing
transfer	transfe**rr**ed	transfe**rr**ing
occur	occu**rr**ed	occu**rr**ing

Exercise 8.5

For each of the following words, use the correctly spelled '-ed' and '-ing' forms of these verbs in sentences of your own. Write two sentences for each root word.

recur	infer	defer	bar	refer

Learn the spelling of these ten words. They are all used in the three passages above:

surrounding	intermittently	wistfully	tongue	puncturing
destination	occasionally	business	assess	government

Vocabulary

Minfong Ho uses the word 'parched' to describe the ground (line 55). How many other words and phrases can you find in the three passages which mean 'very dry'? Then use a thesaurus, either in book form or on a computer, to see how many more words with a similar meaning you can add.

Exercise 8.6

A 'vulnerable' person is at risk. It is derived (comes) from the Latin word *vulnerare*, meaning 'to wound'. Use the following adjectives, all derived from Latin, in sentences of your own. Write in brackets after each one which Latin word it comes from. A good English dictionary will give you this information:

1.	culpable	6.	caprine
2.	hostile	7.	belligerent
3.	pugnacious	8.	sedentary
4.	puerile	9.	military
5.	fraternal	10.	veracious

Grammar and punctuation

A basic English sentence usually begins with the subject (underlined in the examples below), followed by a verb (in **blue**) after which there may be an object or various constructions (in brackets).

> Her sister **ignored** (her).

> The sun **rose** (upon the right).

> People **have** (rights).

> I **enjoyed** (the poem).

> Jinda **laughed**.

However, if a writer shapes too many sentences in this basic way, it makes the writing seem very flat and monotonous. So, to make your writing lively and interesting, you need to experiment with the order of the words (syntax) and to find ways of holding back the subject. Look at these examples:

> Sighing, she **bent** (to work).

> Across the valley, yellow rice fields **stretched**, (stooped and dry).

> Before Astha's involvement, the illiterate and geographically remote people of Kundal **did not know** (their rights).

Day after day, day after day,
<u>We</u> **stuck**, (nor breath nor motion;
As idle as a painted ship
Upon a painted ocean).

In each case the **fronted phrase** – the words which come before the subject – tells you more about the subject.

Each example could be rearranged to put the subject at the front.

Exercise 8.7

Write out the four examples above. Then write them again, but this time start each with the subject. Be careful not to change the meaning.

Decide which sentence you think is better – the original one or yours. Be sure you have a well thought-out reason for your opinion.

Exercise 8.8

Using the following fronted phrases, write complete sentences by adding a subject, a verb and anything else you wish:

1. Together
2. After the storm
3. For many years
4. Near our school
5. Armed with a broom
6. Puzzled
7, Beneath the flames
8. In the morning light

You can be very inventive with adjectives, if you put two words together and link them with a hyphen:

> **Burmese-born** Minfong Ho sets her novel in Thailand.

> The **drought-cursed** village of Kundal is in northern India.

> Coleridge's **thirst-maddened** mariner has sailed all over the world.

Using an original, hyphenated adjective often means you can express your ideas colourfully but in fewer words.

Exercise 8.9

Use your own invented, hyphenated adjectives to complete these sentences:

1. _____ Thailand is in south-east Asia.

2. *The Rime of the Ancient Mariner* is the longest poem in my _____ anthology.

3. Many _____ tourists visit Udaipur.

4. I am tired of ____ television programmes.

5. Access to ____ water is a basic human right.

6. Imagine our ____ at break, smiling over their coffee.

Speaking and listening

1. With your teacher's permission, invite into school a speaker from a charity such as Oxfam to talk to your class about drought in Africa or India. One of you should introduce him or her and another should propose a vote of thanks at the end.

2. Prepare an assembly about drought.

3. What does 'drought' mean in Britain and how does it affect people's lives? Discuss this in groups.

4. Devise a playlet set in a village in a hot country suffering from drought. Show it to the rest of the class.

5. Prepare a rehearsed reading of the extract from *The Rime of the Ancient Mariner* printed in this chapter. Perform it as movingly as you can.

Have you read?

These books all feature drought or journeys on water:

Rice Without Rain by Minfong Ho (1986)
The Rime of the Ancient Mariner by Samuel Taylor Coleridge (1798)
The Clay Marble by Minfong Ho (1989)
Drought by J G Ballard (1981)
Pigeon Post by Arthur Ransome (1936)
Holes by Louis Sacher (2001)
The Land by Mildred D Taylor (2002)
The Wind Caller's Children by Amanda Cockrell (1996)
The Great Elephant Chase by Gillian Cross (1992)
Life of Pi by Yann Martel (2003)
The African Queen by C S Forrester (1935)
The Bible, *Genesis* Chapters 37-50, for the story of Joseph.

And if you've done all that

- Research the albatross. Use reference books or the Internet to find out where it occurs, its appearance, food, habitat and breeding. Put your information onto a poster for the classroom wall.

- Construct a timeline for the life of Samuel Taylor Coleridge (1772-1834). Plot on it wars, kings, events, books published, music written, discoveries and inventions made and anything else which interests you.

- Read the rest of *The Rime of the Ancient Mariner*. Work out – perhaps in a group – how you might stage it as a mime or a play with words.

- Organise a fund-raising event to support a drought-related project. You could ask Christian Aid for advice.

Chapter 9

Bullying

David Copperfield has been placed at Salem House, a boarding school in London. His tyrannical stepfather, Mr Murdstone, wants him out of the way after an argument which ended in David's biting Murdstone's hand. At school, David is forced to wear a placard on his back which says 'Take care of him: He bites'. This is David's first meeting with the headmaster.

1   The wooden-legged man turned me about so as to exhibit the placard; and having afforded time for a full survey of it, turned me about again with my face to Mr Creakle, and posted himself at Mr Creakle's side. Mr Creakle's face was fiery and his eyes were small, and deep in his head; he had thick veins in his forehead, a little nose and a large
5   chin. He was bald on the top of his head: and had some thin wet-looking hair that was just turning grey, brushed across each temple, so that the two sides interlaced on his forehead. But the circumstance about him which impressed me most was that he had no voice but spoke in a whisper. The exertion this cost him, or the consciousness of talking in that feeble way, made his angry face so much more angry, and his thick veins so
10   much thicker when he spoke, that I am not surprised, on looking back, at this peculiarity striking me as his chief one.

'Now,' said Mr Creakle. 'What's the report of this boy?'

'There's nothing against him yet,' returned the man with the wooden leg. 'There has been no opportunity.'

15   I thought Mr Creakle was disappointed. I thought Mrs and Miss Creakle (at whom I now glanced for the first time and who were, both, thin and quiet) were not disappointed.

'Come here Sir!' said Mr Creakle, beckoning to me.

'Come here!' said the man with the wooden leg, repeating the gesture.

20   'I have the happiness of knowing your father-in-law,' whispered Mr Creakle, taking me by the ear; 'and a worthy man he is, and a man of strong character. He knows me and I know him. Do you know me? Hey?' said Mr Creakle, pinching my ear with ferocious playfulness.

'Not yet, Sir', I said, flinching with the pain.

25   'Not yet? Hey?' repeated Mr Creakle. 'But you will soon. Hey?'

'You will soon. Hey?' repeated the man with the wooden leg. I afterwards found that he generally acted, with his strong voice, as Mr Creakle's interpreter to the boys.

I was very much frightened, and said I hoped so, if he pleased. I felt, all this while, as if my ear were blazing; he pinched it so hard.

30 'I'll tell you what I am,' whispered Mr Creakle, letting go at last, with a screw at parting that brought water into my eyes. 'I'm a Tartar.'

'A Tartar,' said the man with the wooden leg.

'When I say I'll do a thing, I do it and when I say I will have a thing done, I will have it done.'

35 '. . . will have a thing done, I will have it done,' repeated the man with the wooden leg.

'I am a determined character,' said Mr Creakle. 'That's what I am. I do my duty. That's what I do. My flesh and blood,' – he looked at Mrs Creakle as he said this – 'when it rises against me is not my flesh and blood. I discard it. Has that fellow' – to the man with the wooden leg – 'been here again?'

40 'No,' was the answer.

'No,' said Mr Creakle. 'He knows better. He knows me. Let him keep away. I say let him keep away,' said Mr Creakle, striking his hand upon the table and looking at Mrs Creakle. 'For he knows me. Now you have begun to know me too, my young friend, and you may go. Take him away.'

45 I was very glad to be ordered away, for Mrs and Miss Creakle were both wiping their eyes, and I felt as uncomfortable for them as I did for myself. But I had a petition on my mind which concerned me so nearly, that I couldn't help saying, though I wondered at my own courage:

'If you please, Sir . . .?'

50 Mr Creakle whispered, 'Hah! What's this?' and bent his eyes upon me as if he would have burnt me up with them.

'If you please, Sir?' I faltered. 'If I might be allowed (I am very sorry indeed, sir, for what I did) to take this writing off, before the boys come back . . .'

55   Whether Mr Creakle was in earnest, or whether he only did it to frighten me, I don't know, but he made a burst out of his chair, before which I precipitately retreated without waiting for the escort of the man with the wooden leg, and never once stopped until I reached my own bedroom where, finding I was not pursued, I went to bed, as it was time, and lay quaking for a couple of hours.

(From *David Copperfield* by Charles Dickens, 1850)

Exercise 9.1

Answer these questions as fully as you can:

1.   How many people were present at this interview?

2.   Who were they?

3.   Why do you think Mr Creakle didn't see his new pupil alone?

4.   What do you learn about Mr Creakle's wife and daughter from this passage?

5.   Give another word which means approximately the same as (a) Tartar (line 31), (b) discard (line 38), (c) faltered (line 52), (d) precipitately (line 55).

6.   Who is being bullied? (Think very carefully about this.)

7.   Sum up in your own words the narrator's feelings after the interview.

Ozymandias

1   I met a traveller from an antique land
     Who said: 'Two vast and trunkless legs of stone
     Stand in the desert. Near them, on the sand,
     Half sunk, a shattered visage lies, whose frown
5   And wrinkled lip, and sneer of cold command,
     Tell that its sculptor well those passions read
     Which yet survive, stamped on those lifeless things,
     The hand that mocked them and the heart that fed;
     And on the pedestal these words appear:
10   "My name is Ozymandias, King of Kings:
     Look on my works, ye Mighty and despair!"
     Nothing beside remains. Round the decay
     Of that colossal wreck, boundless and bare
     The lone and level sands stretch far away.'

(Percy Bysshe Shelley, 1792-1822)

Poetry technique: Consonance

Sometimes poets and writers choose words because they have consonants within them which mirror, match or chime with those in other words nearby. This is called **consonance**.

Consider: 'Half sunk, a shattered visage lies whose frown' (line 4)

The five 's' sounds in the line are an example of consonance. They give the words a hiss of menace.

This is different from **rhyme**, because the consonants can come anywhere in the words, rather than simply at the end. It is different, too, from **alliteration**, which applies to sounds at the beginnings of words. Poets often blend rhyme, alliteration and consonance together.

Remember that all these techniques depend on **sound,** not spelling.

Exercise 9.2

Read the poem *Ozymandias* on page 100 and then answer the following questions:

1.   Who is the narrator of the poem?

2.   Describe the remains of the statue in the desert in your own words.

3.   Give a word which means the same as (a) trunkless (line 2), (b) visage (line 4).

4.   What interests you about the last two lines of the poem?

Consonance: words sharing a consonant

5.   Why do you think this poem has been included in a chapter focusing on bullying?

Bullying – Don't Suffer in Silence. Information for parents and families

1   Every school is likely to have some problem with bullying at one time or another. Your child's school must by law have an anti-bullying policy, and use it to reduce and prevent bullying, as many schools have already successfully done.

   Bullying behaviour includes:

5   ● name calling and nasty teasing

     ● threats and extortion

     ● physical violence

     ● damage to belongings

- leaving pupils out of social activities deliberately and frequently

10   ●   spreading malicious rumours

Parents and families have an important part to play in helping schools deal with bullying.

First, discourage your child from using bullying behaviour at home or elsewhere. Show how to resolve difficult situations without using violence or aggression.

Second, ask to see the school's anti-bullying policy. Each school must have an anti-
15   bullying policy which sets out how it deals with incidents of bullying. You have a right to know about this policy which is as much for parents as for staff and pupils.

Third, watch out for signs that your child is being bullied, or is bullying others. Parents and families are often the first to detect symptoms of bullying, though sometimes school nurses or doctors may first suspect that a child has been bullied. Common symptoms
20   include headaches, stomach aches, anxiety and irritability. It can be helpful to ask questions about progress and friends at school; how break times and lunchtimes are spent; and whether your child is facing problems or difficulties at school. Don't dismiss negative signs. Contact the school immediately if you are worried.

If your child has been bullied:

25   ●   calmly talk to your child about it

- make a note of what your child says – particularly who was said to be involved; how often the bullying has occurred; where it happened and what has happened

- reassure your child that telling you about the bullying was the right thing to do

- explain that any further incidents should be reported to a teacher immediately

30   ●   make an appointment to see your child's class teacher or form tutor

- explain to the teacher the problems your child is experiencing

Talking to teachers about bullying:

- try and stay calm – bear in mind that the teacher may have no idea that your child is being bullied or may have heard conflicting accounts of an incident

35   ●   be as specific as possible about what your child says has happened – give dates, places and names of other children involved

- make a note of what action the school intends to take

- ask if there is anything you can do to help your child or the school

- stay in touch with the school – let them know if things improve as well as if
40   problems continue

If you think your concerns are not being addressed:

- check the school anti-bullying policy to see if agreed procedures are being followed

- discuss your concerns with the parent governor or other parents

- make an appointment to meet the head teacher, keeping a record of the meeting

45
- if this does not help, write to the Chair of Governors explaining your concerns and what you would like to see happen

- contact local or national parent support groups for advice

- contact the Director of Education for your authority, who will be able to ensure that the Governors respond to your concerns

50
- contact the Parentline Plus helpline for support and information at any of these stages

- in the last resort, write to the Secretary of State for Education and Skills, but note that it will only be investigated if the child remains on the roll of the school involved

If your child is bullying other children:

Many children may be involved in bullying other pupils at some time or other. Often parents are not aware. Children sometimes bully others because:

55
- they don't know it is wrong

- they are copying older brothers or sisters or other people in the family they admire

- they haven't learnt other, better ways of mixing with their school friends

- their friends encourage them to bully

- they are going through a difficult time and are acting out aggressive feelings

60 **To stop your child bullying others:**

- talk to your child, explaining that bullying is unacceptable and makes others unhappy

- discourage other members of your family from bullying behaviour or from using aggression or force to get what they want

65
- show your child how to join in with other children without bullying

- make an appointment to see your child's class teacher or form tutor; explain to the teacher the problems your child is experiencing; discuss with the teacher how you and the school can stop them bullying others

- regularly check with your child how things are going at school

70
- give your child lots of praise and encouragement when they are co-operative or kind to other people

(From *DfES* website: *Don't Suffer in Silence.*
For more information please visit www.dfes.gov.uk/bullying

Exercise 9.3

Read the extract from *Bullying – don't suffer in silence*, and then answer the following questions:

1. (a) What is the purpose of this writing? and (b) in what ways is it suitable for that purpose?

2. Why has the writer included so many bullet points?

3. Summarise in your own words, in a short paragraph, the main things which the parents of a child being bullied should do at home.

4. Using your own words, give three reasons why a child might bully others.

5. Why is example important in the prevention of bullying?

6. What would you add to this advice if you were writing it?

Exercise 9.4

Your turn to write:

1. Imagine you are Miss Creakle. You are writing your diary for the day on which you first met David Copperfield. Add as much extra detail of your own as you wish.

2. Write a story or poem of your own about a child who is bullied.

3. Imagine you are the victim of bullying. Write a letter or email to a teacher setting out your problem.

4. Write the text of a newspaper advertisement for a holiday in Egypt, looking at desert sights (and sites!).

5. Why do people become bullies and how can they be helped? Write your views.

Spell check

'dis-' is a prefix. It is added to the fronts of words to give an opposite meaning, although sometimes the meaning has changed so that the two words are no longer the straightforward opposites they once were. So:

appear	**dis**appear
cover	**dis**cover
connect	**dis**connect
continue	**dis**continue
appoint	**dis**appoint
grace	**dis**grace

N.B. LEARN that the 'dis-' prefix has one 's'. So do all the words in this group.

BUT when the root word already begins with 's', adding the 'dis-' prefix produces a double 's'. So:

satisfy	**diss**atisfy
soluble	**diss**oluble
symmetry	**diss**ymmetry
seminate	**diss**eminate

Check that you know how to spell the ten words below, all of which occur in the passages above:

ferocious	whispered	determined	antique	traveller
wrinkled	colossal	successfully	aggression	experiencing

Vocabulary

A 'petition' is a request – from the Latin verb *petere*, meaning 'to seek'.

> 'But I had a **petition** in my mind . . . ' says David Copperfield, meaning that there is a favour he wants to ask of Mr Creakle.

That, however, was 1850. Today the word usually means a written (or, often now, emailed) document, signed by a large number of people demanding action from a government or other authority.

It can also mean a kind of prayer which asks for something and it has a special meaning in law: a 'petition for divorce' is the formal action taken by someone, known as the 'petitioner' who is asking the courts to grant him or her a divorce.

It can be used as a verb too:

> The villagers decided **to petition** for a change in the law.

The adjectival form is 'petitionary':

> The vicar led us in a **petitionary** prayer.

Exercise 9.5

A 'pedestal' is something which is stood on. It comes from the Latin word *pes, ped-*, meaning 'a foot'.

Look up the meanings of the following words and then use them in sentences of your own:

1.	podium	6.	pediform
2.	quadruped	7.	podiatry
3.	arthropod	8.	pedicab
4.	pedicure	9.	centipede
5.	pedometer	10.	tripod

Grammar and punctuation

In Chapter 8, we looked at fronted phrases. Here we learn about **fronted clauses**.

The difference between a clause and a phrase is easy to understand. **A clause contains one or more verbs** which have a clear tense (known as **finite verbs**). **A phrase has no finite verb**.

As with the fronted phrases in Chapter 8, fronted clauses are a way of delaying the subject of the sentence and the main verb. That helps writers to vary the shapes of their sentences. A fronted clause often needs a comma after it before the main sentence begins.

Look at these examples of fronted clauses. For clarity in the examples, the fronted clause is marked in **blue** with its own finite verb <u>underlined</u>.

> **Nasty bully as he <u>was</u>**, Mr Creakle was probably a coward at heart.

> **When you <u>are waiting</u> at a bus stop**, you don't expect to see the Queen driving past.

> **After noticing that his watch <u>was missing</u>**, Mr Swynford notified the police.

> **Because I <u>love</u> pears**, I bought a whole kilo at the supermarket.

> **A brave woman who <u>is</u> not afraid to speak her mind**, Mrs Smithers angrily confronted the intruder.

Exercise 9.6

Complete these sentences by adding a main sentence to the fronted clause:

1. If a teacher makes the lesson interesting, . . .

2. After Adam had finished his lunch, . . .

3. An impulsive girl who rarely thought ahead, . . .

4. Once his prep was given in, . . .

5. Because I enjoyed *David Copperfield*, . . .

6. A statue which lies in ruins in the desert, . . .

Exercise 9.7

Add a fronted clause to these sentences. Remember that a clause needs at least one finite verb.

1. . . . , the bully was sent home.

2. . . . , Charles Dickens was a prolific writer.

3. . . . , Mrs Edwards learned to swim.

4.   . . . , you can't help noticing.

5.   . . . , I enjoyed Shelley's famous poem.

6.   . . . , we all left immediately.

Exercise 9.8

Sometimes in English the word order (syntax) changes meaning. Simply reversing two words can make a difference. It's like looking at the words in a mirror. And sometimes in the mirror, the two words, as they were once, have come to be written as one. Look at these examples of this kind of 'mirror':

output	put out
upstart	start up
offcut	cut off

Use these pairs of words in sentences of your own to show you understand their meaning. Write two sentences for each pair.

1.	income	come in
2.	upset	set up
3.	overturn	turn over
4.	helpless	less help
5.	outreach	reach out
6.	outlook	look out

Subordinate clauses

A simple sentence such as 'I like English.' needs no punctuation other than a capital letter at the beginning and a full stop at the end. You can, however, make it more complex by adding **subordinate** (secondary) **clauses**. These are also known as **dependent** (hanging) **clauses**. If you do this, you will need to divide them from the main sentence with commas. Think of the main sentence as a closed box. Commas can be used only inside the box. So:

> Because I had a wonderful teacher in my prep school, I like English, which gives me huge amounts of pleasure, especially when we read classic books that I wouldn't otherwise have known about.

Four subordinate statements have been included:

> I had a wonderful teacher in my prep school. (fronted clause)

> English gives me huge amounts of pleasure.

> We read classic books.

> I wouldn't otherwise have known about (them).

You need the commas to make sense of this complex sentence. They act like sign posts.

Exercise 9.9

Add as many subordinate clauses as you can to these basic sentences, using commas where you need them:

1. My school is small.

2. Dickens wrote many novels.

3. Our headmistress has introduced an anti-bullying policy.

4. Shelley died in 1822.

5. Eat healthily.

6. Mr Creakle bullied David Copperfield.

Speaking and listening

1. Interview someone over 50 about bullying in schools in the past. Discuss attitudes to bullying today with a teacher at your school and with some other pupils. Write an article on the interview for your school magazine about how attitudes have changed.

2. Work out a role play with two other people. One of you is a bully and one is a victim. The third person is another pupil or a teacher who stops the bullying. Try this several times so that you each try out each of the roles.

3. Prepare a short talk for your class about either the novels of Charles Dickens or schools in the 1850s. If you like, and if it is possible, this could be a Power Point presentation.

Have you read?

All these books relate to the theme of bullying:

David Copperfield by Charles Dickens (1850)
Nicholas Nickleby by Charles Dickens (1839)
Tom Brown's Schooldays by Thomas Hughes (1857)
I'm the King of the Castle by Susan Hill (1974)
The Chocolate War by Robert Cormier (1974)
Fat Boy Swim by Catherine Forde (2003)
The Bailey Game by Celia Rees (2002)
Chicken by Alan Gibbons (1993)
Malarkey by Keith Grave (2003)
Playing it Cool by Jacqueline Roy (1998)
The Protectors by Pete Johnson (1998)

And if you've done all that

- Use the Internet and/or reference books to find out what you can about the short but colourful life of Percy Bysshe Shelley.

- As we learnt on page 60, **phrasal verbs** are verbs which – with a specific adverb and/or preposition – have taken on a new meaning. 'Put up with' means 'tolerate' and 'put off' means 'postpone'; 'stand up for' means 'support'; 'turn down' means 'reject' but 'turn up' means 'arrive'. List as many examples as you can. Start with 'run' (in, up, down etc). Other everyday root verbs are 'take' and 'push,' but there are many more. Make sure you know what they mean. Some (think about 'take off') have more than one meaning.

- Find the 1964 poem *The Place's Fault* by Philip Hobsbaum. It's in many anthologies. Read it carefully several times. Make up some questions about the poem and try them out on someone else in the class. Decide whether, if you had been writing this chapter of this book, you would have used *The Place's Fault* as a passage to study rather than *Ozymandias* and, if so, why?

Chapter 10

Animals

Hazel is leading his group of rabbits on a long journey to the safety of a new home on Watership Down. Suddenly there is danger.

1   Hazel thought quickly. If the fox were not too close, all they had to do was run. There was woodland nearby and they could vanish into it, keeping more or less together, and simply continue on their way. He pushed through the burdocks.

'How close is it?' he asked. 'And where's Fiver?'

5   'I'm here,' replied Fiver, from a few yards away. He was squatting under the long briars of a dog-rose and did not turn his head as Hazel came up beside him. 'And there's the fox,' he added. Hazel followed his gaze.

The rough weed-covered grounds of the combe sloped away below them, a long dip bounded on the north by Caesar's Belt. The last of the setting sun shone straight up it

10   through a break in the trees. The fox was below them and still some way off. Although it was almost directly downwind and must therefore be able to smell them, it did not look as though it were particularly interested in rabbits. It was trotting steadily up the combe like a dog, trailing its white-tipped brush. In colour it was sandy brown, with dark legs and ears. Even now, though obviously not hunting, it had a crafty, predatory

15   look that made the watchers among the dog-roses shiver. As it passed behind a patch of thistles and disappeared from view, Hazel and Fiver returned to the others.

'Come on,' said Hazel. 'If you've never seen a fox don't bother to go and look now. Just follow me.'

He was about to lead the way up the south side of the combe, when suddenly a rabbit

20   shouldered him roughly aside, pushed past Fiver and was gone into the open. Hazel stopped and looked round in amazement.

'Who was that?' he asked.

'Bigwig,' answered Fiver, staring.

Together they went quickly back to the briars and once more looked into the combe.

25   Bigwig, in full view, was loping wearily downhill, straight towards the fox. They watched him aghast. He drew near, but still the fox paid no attention.

'Hazel,' said Silver from behind, 'shall I . . .?'

'No one is to move,' said Hazel quickly. 'Keep still all of you.'

30 At about thirty yards' distance the fox saw the approaching rabbit. It paused for a moment and then continued to trot forwards. It was almost upon him before Bigwig turned and began to limp up the north slope of the combe towards the trees of the Belt. The fox hesitated and then followed him.

'What's he up to?' muttered Blackberry.

'Trying to draw it off, I suppose,' replied Fiver.

35 'But he didn't have to. We'd have got away without that.'

'Confounded fool!' said Hazel. 'I don't know when I've been so angry.'

The fox had quickened its pace and was now some distance away from them. It appeared to be overtaking Bigwig. The sun had set and in the failing light they could just make him out as he entered the undergrowth. He disappeared and the fox followed.
40 For several moments all was quiet. Then horribly clear across the darkening, empty combe there came the agonising squeal of a stricken rabbit.

'O Frith and Inlé!' cried Blackberry, stamping. Pipkin turned to bolt. Hazel did not move.

'Shall we go, Hazel?' asked Silver. 'We can't help him now'

As he spoke, Bigwig suddenly broke out of the trees, running very fast. Almost before
45 they could grasp that he was alive, he had recrossed the entire upper slope of the combe in a single dash and bolted in among them.

'Come on,' said Bigwig, 'let's get out of here!'

'But what – what – are you wounded?' asked Bluebell in bewilderment.

'No,' said Bigwig. 'Never better! Let's go!'

50 'You can wait until I'm ready', said Hazel in a cold, angry tone. 'You've done your best to kill yourself and acted like a complete fool. Now hold your tongue and sit down.' He turned and, although it was rapidly becoming too dark to see any distance, made as though he were still looking out across the combe. Behind him, the rabbits fidgeted nervously.

(From *Watership Down* by Richard Adams, 1972)

Exercise 10.1

Answer the following questions as fully as you can:

1. What time of day is it and how can you tell?

2. What exactly did Bigwig do?

3. What do you learn about Hazel's leadership skills from this passage?

4. Find expressions in the passage which mean (a) was accelerating, (b) in dismay, (c) untrustworthy appearance.

5. Explain why Hazel is angry with Bigwig.

Encounters with Animals

Naturalist and founder of Jersey Zoo, Gerald Durrell describes how, as a boy, he adopted a family of orphaned hedgehogs.

1   The first real attempt I made at being a foster-mother was to four baby hedgehogs. The female hedgehog is a very good mother. She constructs an underground nursery for the reception of her young: a circular chamber about a foot below ground level, lined with a thick layer of dry leaves. Here she gives birth to her babies which are blind and

5   helpless. They are covered with a thick layer of spikes, but these are white and soft as though made of rubber. They gradually harden and turn brown when the babies are a few weeks old. When they are old enough to leave the nursery, the mother leads them out and shows them how to hunt for food. They walk in line rather like a school crocodile, the tail of one held in the mouth of the baby behind. The baby at the head of

10   the column holds tight to the mother's tail with grim determination and they wend their way through the twilit hedgerows like a strange and prickly centipede.

     To a mother hedgehog the rearing of her babies seems to present no problems. But when I was suddenly presented with four blind, white, rubbery-spiked babies to rear, I was not so sure. We were living in Greece at the time, and the nest, which was about the size of

15   a football and made of oak leaves, had been dug up by a peasant working in his fields. The first job was to feed the babies, for the ordinary baby's feeding bottle only took a teat far too large for their tiny mouths. Luckily, the young daughter of a friend of mine had a doll's feeding bottle and after much bribery I got her to part with it. After a time the hedgehogs took to this and thrived on a diet of diluted cow's milk.

20   I kept them at first in a shallow cardboard box where I had put the nest. But in record time the original nest was so unhygienic that I found myself having to change the leaves ten or twelve times a day. I began to wonder if the mother hedgehog spent her day rushing to and fro with piles of fresh leaves to keep her nest clean, and, if she did, how on earth she found time to satisfy the appetites of her babies. Mine were always ready

25   for food at any time of day or night. You only had to touch the box and a chorus of shrill screams arose from four little pointed faces poking out of the leaves, each head decorated with a crew cut of white spikes; and the little black noses would whiffle desperately from side to side in an effort to locate the bottle.

     Most baby animals know when they have had enough, but in my experience this does

30   not apply to baby hedgehogs. Like four survivors from a raft, they flung themselves on to the bottle and sucked and sucked and sucked as if they had not had a decent meal in weeks. If I had allowed it they would have drunk twice as much as was good for them. As it was I think I tended to overfeed them, for their tiny legs could not support the weight of their fat bodies and they would advance across the carpet with a curious

35   swimming motion, their tummies dragging on the ground. However, they progressed

very well: their legs grew stronger, their eyes opened and they would even make daring excursions as much as six inches away from their box.

I was very proud of my prickly family.

(From *Encounters with Animals* by Gerald Durrell, 1958)

Exercise 10.2

Now answer the following questions:

1. Summarise in your own words the ways in which a female hedgehog is a 'good mother'.

2. Which three characteristics distinguish baby hedgehogs from adults?

3. Which two aspects of hedgehog behaviour made the writer's job difficult?

4. What evidence is there that the writer was overfeeding his 'prickly family'.

5. Gerald Durrell is known as a humorous writer. Pick two examples of wittiness in the language he uses here and explain why you chose them.

The Tyger

1   Tyger! Tyger! burning bright
In the forests of the night,
What immortal hand or eye
Could frame thy fearful symmetry?

5   In what distant deeps or skies
Burnt the fire of thine eyes?
On what wings dare he aspire?
What the hand dare seize the fire?

And what shoulder, and what art
10   Could twist the sinews of thy heart?
And, when thy heart began to beat,
What dread hand? And what dread feet?

What the hammer? What the chain?
In what furnace was thy brain?
15   What the anvil? What dread grasp
Does its deadly terrors clasp?

When the stars threw down their spears,
And water'd heaven with their tears,
Did he smile his work to see?
Did he who made the lamb make thee?

Tyger! Tyger! burning bright
In the forests of the night,
What immortal hand or eye
Dare frame thy fearful symmetry?

(William Blake, 1757-1827)

Poetry technique: Assonance

Assonance is similar to consonance, except that it's the **vowel** sounds which match.

Tyger tyger burning bright

eyes as wide as a football pool

wrinkled lip

I hate a wasted journey

When Blake writes:

In what distant deeps or skies
Burned the fire of thine eyes?

or Charles Causley writes:

Deep in the sand they silently sank
And each struck a match for the petrol tank.

Assonance: words sharing a vowel

he is blending rhyme, alliteration, consonance and assonance. Can you see how it works? Remember to listen to the sounds and ignore the spelling.

The Ancient Greeks regarded poetry as a form of music. Do you think they were right?

Exercise 10.3

Study *The Tyger* and answer the following questions:

1.   Whom is the narrator addressing?

2.   What do you think the poet means by 'fearful symmetry' (line 24)?

3.   Why is the lamb mentioned?

4.   What is the meaning of (a) aspire (line 7), (b) sinews (line 10), (c) anvil (line 15)?

5.   Why do you think the poet repeats the word 'dread' (lines 12 and 15)?

6.   In what ways is this a religious poem?

Exercise 10.4

Your turn to write:

1.   Write an article for a wildlife magazine, explaining how to care for orphaned hedgehogs.

2.   Think of an animal which inspires awe, fear, wonder or admiration (or any mixture of these) in you. Write a poem addressed to that animal expressing your feelings.

3.   Research and write a short biography (really a biographical essay) of William Blake.

4.   Write a story in which a group of animals is dealing with conflict.

5.   Write about animals in any way you wish.

6.   Write an account of your own experiences entitled 'Encounters with Animals'. If you can make it amusing as Gerald Durrell does, so much the better.

7.   Imagine you are some sort of animal. Tell a story from your point of view.

Spell check

'**-al**' and '**-le**'

Some people confuse words ending in '-cal' and '-cle' because they sound almost the same. Remember that '-cal' words are adjectives and '-cle' words are nouns. Then it's quite easy. For example:

adjectives: '-cal'	**nouns**: '-cle'
vocal	receptacle
practical	vehicle
logical	obstacle
musical	article
physical	miracle

The same is true of words like '**princi**pal' and '**princi**ple' and you need to take special care with them.

N.B. The 'Principal' of a college is the principal lecturer, hence the spelling. A 'musical' is a musical entertainment, hence the spelling. In both cases, we are really using a shortened form, which is why the word is spelled as an adjective, although grammatically it's used as a noun.

'**-se**' and '**-ce**'

'advise' is a **verb**:

I advise you to look up the facts.

'advice' is a **noun**:

Mrs Jefferson gave Tim her advi**ce**.

This is fairly easy because 'advise' and 'advice' are pronounced differently in spoken English. 'Devise' and 'device' work in the same way.

Use this as a way of helping you to spell correctly a small group of related words which many people get wrong in writing because some of them sound the same in speech:

verbs: '-s-'	nouns: '-c-'
advise	advice
devise	device
license	licence
practise	practice
prophesy	prophecy

Beware of American spelling, which occurs in books published in the USA, in films or on the Internet etc., and does not make this distinction. Nonetheless, it is important that you get it right in British English.

Finally, while we are thinking about spelling, check that you know the spellings of these ten words, all of which are used in this chapter:

particularly	amazement	approaching	fidgeted	chorus
unhygienic	desperately	progressed	immortal	symmetry

Exercise 10.5

Put the correct spellings into these:

1.   a historic_____ novel

2.   the mirac_____ of the loaves and fishes

3.   a new bicyc_____

4.   physic_____ education

5.   Archimedes's princip_____

6.   a hysteric_____ laugh.

Exercise 10.6

Fill in the gaps in these sentences:

1.   I like to pract_____ the piano.

2.   Elijah began to proph_____.

3.   I shall apply for a provisional driving lic_____ as soon as I'm seventeen.

4. Hockey pract____ is my favourite activity.

5. I must lic____ my television set.

6. There is a lot of proph____ in the Bible.

Vocabulary

The fox in *Watership Down* 'loped'. This is a **verb of movement** like 'ran', 'walked', 'strolled' and 'galloped'. Make a list of as many verbs of movement as you can, writing them down in their past tense, '-ed' form. Try to use some of the less obvious ones in your own writing when it's appropriate.

The verb 'aspire' (usually with the preposition to) means 'to yearn', 'to have a powerful or ambitious plan' or 'to hope to do something':

> He aspires to be a great leader.

The related noun is 'aspiration' and the adjective 'aspirational'. They all come from the Latin verb *spirare*, meaning 'to breathe'.

Exercise 10.7

Look up the meanings of these related words and use them in sentences of your own:

1. inspire
2. expire

3. transpire
4. conspire

Grammar and punctuation

A **gerund** is a noun formed from a verb by adding '-ing'. So:

> The **going** is tough
> Do you like **singing**?
> **Swimming** doesn't appeal to me.

A **gerundive** is an adjective (remember they both end in '-ive') formed from a verb by adding '-ing'. So:

> The **parking** space is too small.
> **Driving** lessons are fun.
> **Cooking** apples are sour.

A gerund chasing a gerundive

Exercise 10.8

1. Use the following words in sentences of your own. Write in brackets after each whether you have used it as a gerund or a gerundive:

   eating   playing   walking   shopping   riding   falling

2. Now write another six sentences using the same words. Where you used a gerund before, now use a gerundive and vice versa. Write in brackets after each what it is.

Exercise 10.9

To revise (and test) all the punctuation which you have learned, write out these paragraphs, taking care to punctuate each one correctly:

1. the sea lifted smooth blue muscles of wave as it stirred in the dawn light and the foam of our wake spread gently behind us like a white peacocks tail glinting with bubbles the sky was pale and stained with yellow on the eastern horizon ahead lay a chocolate brown smudge of land huddled in mist with a frill of foam at its base this was corfu and we strained our eyes to make out the exact shapes of the mountains to discover valleys peaks ravines and beaches but it remained a silhouette

   (From *My Family and Other Animals* by Gerald Durrell, 1956)

2. that's polly pig she said pointing to the sow nuzzling the straw in its pen she's mine my dad gave her to me i leaned over the pen yes i know youre a lucky girl she looks a fine pig to me oh she is she is the little girls eyes shone with pleasure i feed her every day and she lets me stroke her shes nice I bet she is she looks nice yes and do you know something else tesss voice grew serious and her voice took on a conspiratorial tone shes going to have babies in march

   (From *The Lord God Made Them All* by James Herriot, 1981)

Speaking and listening

1. Organise a class discussion – or a formal debate – on an animal-rights subject, such as fox hunting or medical experimentation on animals.

2. Comb anthologies for an animal poem which appeals to you. Practise reading until you feel really confident and then perform it to the class. You might also learn it by heart.

3. Prepare an instructive talk about how to care for a pet. (You will have to decide what the pet is.) Take it in turns to deliver your talks in small groups.

4. With your teacher's consent and help, invite in a speaker from one of the well-known animal charities, such as Cat Protection, RSPCA or Dogs Trust. Interview the visitor in groups, having carefully prepared your questions.

Have you read?

These are all animal stories:

Watership Down by Richard Adams (1972)
The Plague Dogs by Richard Adams (1977)
Encounters With Animals by Gerald Durrell (1958)
Three Singles to Adventure by Gerald Durrell (1962)
Tarka the Otter by Henry Williamson (1927)
Jennie by Paul Gallico (1950)
Thomasina by Paul Gallico (1957)
Blitzcat by Robert Westall (1989)
Duncton Wood by William Horwood (1980)
Ring of Bright Water by Gavin Maxwell (1960)
Zoo Vet by David Taylor (1976)
The Red Pony by John Steinbeck (1937)
If Only They Could Talk by James Herriot (1970)

And if you've done all that

- Look up 'anthropomorphism'. Many writers about animals use it. Collect as many examples as you can, starting, perhaps, with Beatrix Potter who wrote *The Tale of Peter Rabbit*. Work out what you feel about it.

- In *Watership Down*, Richard Adams's rabbits speak a made-up language called Lapine. (Why did he choose to call it that?) To remind us of this he drops words of this fictional language into the story. Make up some vocabulary for a language called Feline, Canine or Caprine. Remember that you only need language for activities and ideas which affect <u>you</u>. In Lapine, for instance, Adams's rabbits go out at dusk every day to 'silflay' – characteristically rabbity grazing. Humans and other animals don't need a word for this!

- ### The Zebras

    From the dark woods that breathe of fallen showers,
    Harnessed with level rays in golden reins
    The Zebras draw the dawn across the plains
    Wading knee-deep among the scarlet flowers.
    The sunlight, zithering their flanks with fire,
    Flashes between the shadows as they pass
    Barred with electric tremors through the grass
    Like wind along the golden strings of a lyre.

    Into the flushed air snorting rosy plumes

That smoulder round their feet in drifting fumes
With dove-like voices call their distant fillies,
While round the herds the stallion wheels his flight,
Engine of beauty volted with delight,
To roll his mare among the trampled lilies.

(Roy Campbell, 1901 – 1957)

- Enjoy the poem above; it's worth reading several times. Use it as a starting point for your own personal anthology of animal poems. Search published selections and collections. Copy or type out the ones you like and keep them in a notebook or ring binder. D H Lawrence's *Snake* or John Masefield's *Reynard the Fox* might appeal to you.

- This book has several times mentioned 'American spelling'. Do you know why it's different? Look up Noah Webster and find out.